Nourish:
An Integrative Medicine Cookbook

Anne Kennard, DO

Copyright 2019 Swiner Publishing Company. All Rights Reserved.
ISBN: 9781697372212

Table of Contents

WELCOME 1

EATING THE RAINBOW: A GUIDE TO PHYTONUTRIENTS .. 3

A NOTE ON FATS 7

DR. K'S GUIDE TO HEALTHY FATS 10

    ANIMAL FATS 10

    FISH 10

    DAIRY 11

    NUTS AND SEEDS 11

    COOKING OILS 11

COOKING WITH OILS 12

WHY ARE YOUR RECIPES GLUTEN-FREE? 14

CHRONIC INFLAMMATION AND "THE LEAKY GUT" .. 16

WHAT ABOUT PROBIOTICS? 19

DR. KENNARD'S KITCHENWARE 22

FOOD AS MEDICINE 25

60-SECOND SIMPLE GREENS 26

BRIGHT LIGHTS SALAD 29

DR. K'S IMMUNE BOOST LENTIL STEW 31

MEDICINAL MUSHROOMS: NATURE'S IMMUNE MODULATOR 34

SWEET POTATO & TURKEY CHILI 37

BONE BROTH 40

BONE BROTH JASMINE RICE 43

ROASTED SPAGHETTI SQUASH CASSEROLE 45

FALL HARVEST ROASTED SQUASH 47

MOROCCAN CHICKEN TAGINE 51

GRATEFUL PIZZA 53

SCARBOROUGH FAIR MEATBALLS 57

COCONUT CHICKEN AND VEGETABLE CURRY 60

SWEET POTATO EGG SKILLET 63

ROASTED ROOT VEGGIES 67

ROOT VEGGIE BUDDHA BOWL 69

WATERMELON CHICKEN TACOS 71

DR. K'S GRAIN-FREE FLOUR BLEND 73

PISTACHIO PUMPKIN APPLE MUFFINS 74

DR. K'S HERBAL POWERBALLS 76

    BASIC POWERBALL RECIPE 77

    TUMMY LOVE POWERBALLS 78

    CACAO IMMUNITY POWERBALLS 79

PALEO DARK CHOCOLATE, COCONUT and SEA SALT
COOKIES 81

BIG SUR GRANOLA 83

OVERNIGHT OATS AND CHIA PARFAIT 87

MEDICINAL SIPS 88

"TIRED AND WIRED" TEA 89

GINGER TEA 93

HOT FLASH SUN TEA 94

BEST REST TEA 96

HONEY "LEMON-AID" 98

HIBISCUS COOLER 100

DR. K'S ANTI-INFLAMMATORY ELIXIR 102

ADAPTOGENIC ALMOND MILK 104

GOLDEN MILK 107

SPICED OAT MILK 109

ENERGIZING RHODIOLA HIBISCUS TEA 111

PREGNANCY AND POSTPARTUM TEA 113

MOON TEA 114

HERBAL MEDICINE 116

THE BASICS: TINCTURES AND GLYCERITES 118

DR. K'S ELDERBERRY ELIXIR 120

ELDERBERRY POPSICLES 123

DR. K'S HERBAL COUGH SYRUP 125

SORE THROAT SALT GARGLE 128

CITRUS SPICED BITTERS AND DIGESTION 130

IMMUNITY OXYMEL ELIXIR 132

INFUSED HONEYS 133

LAVENDER HONEY 134

ADAPTOGEN HONEY 136

SAGE AND THYME HONEY 138

SKIN HONEY 140

PEPPERMINT SKIN COMPRESS 142

NATURAL BODY SCRUB 143

NATURAL DEODORANT 144

THE BASICS: INFUSED OILS 145

THE BASICS: MAKING A SALVE 146

HAPPY SKIN SALVE 148

ECZEMA SALVE 150

COUGH SALVE 152

POSTPARTUM SOAK 153

TOXINS IN THE HOME 155

    PERSONAL CARE PRODUCTS 159

HEALTHY HOME CLEANER 163

NATURAL SOFT SCRUB 164

MIND/BODY MEDICINE 165

THE 4-7-8 BREATH 168

THE THREE-PART BREATH 170

THE CIRCULAR BREATH 171

THE BOX BREATH 172

ENERGY BREATH 173

LEGS UP THE WALL POSE 174

DR. KENNARD'S YIN YOGA FOR SLEEP 175

MEDITATION 177

AWARENESS MEDITATION 180

COUNTED BREATH MEDITATION 181

SIX SENSES MEDITATION 182

MALA MEDITATION 184

LOVING-KINDNESS MEDITATION 185

BEE BREATH MEDITATION 187

FLASHLIGHT MEDITATION 189

ACKNOWLEDGEMENTS 190

WELCOME

Welcome to Nourish: An Integrative Medicine Cookbook. As an Integrative Medicine and OB/GYN physician, herbalist, yoga instructor, nutritionist, and avid cook, these recipes have been developed over time, combining medicinal food and drinks, herbal medicine, and mind-body medicine. As I progressed through my medical training, it became apparent to me that many of the valuable skills I was learning helped patients in acute, life-threatening situations, but we did not have as much to offer for chronic, lifestyle-mediated diseases. I was taught to recognize and treat acute, life-threatening illnesses, but was never taught the answer to a different, very important question: "What makes a person well?"

This book is a compilation of some ideas to try to answer that question. I have used these recipes with patients for years, with happy and delicious success for many. Making medicine, through food, herbs, and mind-body practices, helps to shift the locus of control back to the patient for their own health, empowering them to live in a way that helps wellness to flourish.

This book is named Nourish, because I truly hope that it provides nourishment to the body, mind, and spirit. To care for the whole person is the foundation of Integrative Medicine.

EATING THE RAINBOW: A GUIDE TO PHYTONUTRIENTS

One of the goals of my recipes is to highlight the range of phytonutrients across the rainbow.

Let's explore several types of phytonutrients.

Polyphenols and Flavonoids, containing more than 8000 different phenolic compounds, are nature's biological response modifiers. They perform direct antioxidant, anti-cancer, anti-inflammatory, anti-aging activities in the body. They improve gut microbiota, cell signaling, cognitive function, and cellular detoxification pathways. They also aid in the prevention of disorders of inflammation including cardiovascular disease, type 2 diabetes, and even decrease cancer risk. Some of the most beneficial and anti-inflammatory polyphenols are anthocyanins, found in blue and purple colored plant foods. A notable flavonoid is in green tea. This high antioxidant has been found to be effective in cancer prevention, blood sugar regulation, and dementia prevention. Many of the medicinal plants owe their healing effects to their flavonoid components. Cacao, found in raw dark chocolate, is tremendously high in flavonoids and delicious!

Carotenoids, particularly beneficial for eye, immune, and ovarian health, are present in the orange and yellow colored plant foods. Two common carotenoids, lutein and zeaxanthin, have been found to decrease risk of macular degeneration risk by 43%. Quercetin, beta-cryptoxanthin, and lycopene are other important carotenoids recognized for cellular detoxification, decreased inflammation, and improving prostate health.

Ellagic acid is a phytochemical known for anti-inflammatory and antioxidant properties, found in berries, especially raspberries, grapes, walnuts, pecans, and pomegranates.

Phytoestrogens are phytonutrients including: isoflavones, found in soy and some legumes, and lignans, found in flaxseed and oats. Soy is the most known phytoestrogen, containing the genistin, daidzin, and glycitin isoflavones. These can bind to estrogen receptors, causing a spectrum of effects. While the data is still being studied, my general recommendation is that whole soy foods such as tempeh and edamame can be eaten healthfully, but avoidance of processed soy foods is likely prudent.

Glucosinolates are sulfur-containing compounds responsible for much of the anti-cancer effects of cruciferous vegetables, including broccoli, cauliflower, kale, and Brussels sprouts. The indole-3-carbinol may be responsible for this effect, and the effect is potent; large studies through the National Institute of Health have shown a 23% reduction in many types of cancers, including lung, colon, and breast cancers when these foods are eaten regularly.

Resveratrol, found in primarily grape skins, and wine, is a potent polyphenol, supporting decrease of inflammation, sensitizing cells to insulin, and optimizing heart health.

Of interest, foods provide the best source of phytonutrients, not supplements. While many different diets are debated- vegan, vegetarian, plant-based, ketogenic, Paleo, and more, all types of healthful eating generally include large amounts of fruits and vegetables. This is truly the foundation of viewing Food as Medicine.

A NOTE ON FATS

The paradigm on fat is changing. When I was getting my degree in Nutrition Science, it was very simple. Unsaturated fats were good, and saturated fats were bad. All fat was supposed to be limited. Americans were told to eat less fat, and in response, we saw an explosion of low-fat products on the market. These products were high in carbohydrates, sugars, processed ingredients and artificial sweeteners, "yet were marketed as heart-healthy options."

We have not recovered.

The two decades that followed witnessed a profound spike in diabetes, fatty liver disease and obesity. Carbohydrate consumption spiked. The artificial sweeteners and processed foods altered the healthy gut microbiome, predisposing people to profound metabolic disturbance. This was replicated all over the globe, as more countries adopted a Western diet.

The popular diets of today – the Paleo diet, Whole 30, Ketogenic – they are reflecting a new shift in society. Coconut oil, MCT oil, and grass-fed meat and dairy is all the rage on the Whole Foods shelves, all foods that were previously shunned as being too high in saturated fats. Society is starting to shift towards a healthier attitude towards fat.

We still have residual fear of a fat as a society, but fat is important for many of the physiologic processes of the body, including satiety and metabolism. It's important for pregnant patients to get enough fat to support their bodies while growing a baby. It's even more important during breast-feeding to have adequate fat intake, as the breast milk itself is so high in fat content. Many peri- and post-menopausal patients are frustrated by the change in their metabolism and I always recommend an increase in healthy fat to stabilize blood sugar and quell cravings. Healthy fats are protective against disorders of inflammation, diabetes, obesity, Alzheimer's and even depression. In fact, fats such as potent eicosapentaenoic acid are now being used as supplemental agents in treatments for autoimmune conditions, heart disease and depression. Docosahexaenoic acid is a vital supplement during pregnancy and lactation for infant brain and eye development.

What is one to do with all of this information? Increase fat intake. It's time for us to embrace fat as a vital nutrient and consume it accordingly, emphasizing healthy oils, avocados, nuts and limited amounts of grass-fed dairy and meat. Trans fats and fried foods should be completely avoided.

DR. K'S GUIDE TO HEALTHY FATS

This list is a balanced recommendation taking into account nutritional considerations as well as the welfare of animals and our planet:

ANIMAL FATS
Emphasize grass-fed beef and game meats, pastured and organic poultry and omega-3 enriched pastured eggs
Avoid conventionally raised beef, feedlot animals, charred meats, meat preserved with nitrites, and conventional poultry

FISH
- Emphasize small to medium size fatty fish including salmon, trout, sardines, herring and halibut.
- Reference the Monterey Bay Aquarium's Seafood.
- Watch for sustainability at *seafoodwatch.org*.

Avoid high-mercury fish and fish susceptible to overfishing, notably swordfish, shark, tilefish, tuna

DAIRY

Emphasize organic, grass-fed butter and ghee, organic, grass-fed full-fat milk and cream, full fat yogurt without added sweeteners and sheep and goat's milk cheeses

Ghee, goat's and sheep's milk products are often better tolerated than cow's milk products

Avoid conventionally raised dairy, nonfat products and products with added sugars

NUTS AND SEEDS

Emphasize walnuts, almonds, flaxseed (ground and stored in freezer), Brazil nuts, hazelnuts, pecans, pistachios, chia seeds, all-natural nut butters

Avoid peanut butters with added palm oils, sugar and soy protein isolate

COOKING OILS

Emphasize, depending on the temperature of cooking, coconut oil, olive oil, avocado oil and grapeseed oil

Avoid sunflower oil, safflower oil, corn oil, canola oil, hydrogenated or partially hydrogenated oils, margarine and shortening

COOKING WITH OILS

Oils are not created equal in terms of cooking safety. Once an oil begins to smoke, it has become oxidized and has created extremely inflammatory compounds that are harmful to ingest. Burned food in general is not healthy (or tasty!), such as the "char" that meat gets on a grill. Charred foods are clearly pro-carcinogenic (strongly associated with stomach and colon cancers) and should not be consumed. Care should be taken to select an oil that fits your cooking temperature needs.

Olive oil, while terrifically healthy, has a relatively low smoke point and therefore should only be used to cook foods at relatively low temperatures or used as a "finish" on a meat, fish or vegetables. Avocado, coconut and grapeseed oils along with ghee have higher smoke points and are more appropriate oils for cooking or grilling. Any oil will oxidize and become inflammatory oil when fried; this is the reason why fried foods are some of the most harmful foods on the planet and should be completely avoided.

I prefer 'cold-pressed' or 'expeller-pressed' oils when possible. This oil did not undergo a chemical solvent for extraction. Industrial refined vegetable oils like soybean and corn oils are typically extracted using toxic chemical solvents, such as hexane, to yield increased output. The chemical residue remains in the food.

OIL	SMOKE POINT (Fahrenheit)
Flaxseed oil	225
Olive oil, extra virgin	320
Butter	350
Sesame oil	350
Grapeseed oil	420
Coconut oil	450
Ghee (clarified butter)	480
Avocado oil	520

WHY ARE YOUR RECIPES GLUTEN-FREE?

I started to have a gluten-free kitchen when my husband was diagnosed with celiac disease, an autoimmune condition triggered by gluten and treated with a gluten-free diet. How marvelous to have full treatment of a chronic illness just by food alone! Our kitchen became gluten-free overnight and I had to learn how to turn my avid baking hobby into something that was compatible with this diet and still tasted good.

I started to learn more about gluten and its effects on the body after I noticed a flare up of my own autoimmune symptoms any time I indulged in a wheat-y treat. And what I've concluded after seeing thousands of patients with multiple, chronic complaints, is that for everyone – not just someone with an autoimmune disease – gluten is not a friend.

Over the last century, gluten content in American grain has increased and these "franken-wheats" are nearly universal. (This explains why some folks who feel effects in U.S. are okay eating bread in Europe). Gluten causes gut inflammation, triggering increased gut permeability (see "Leaky Gut") and can precipitate or aggravate autoimmune conditions, irritable bowel syndrome, small intestinal bacterial overgrowth, joint pain, general fatigue, "brain fog", inability to lose weight and negatively affect thyroid function.

Almost all patients that I have suggested try a gluten-free diet have come back to me with a report of improvement of their symptoms. To see if it is right for you, completely eliminate gluten for at least three weeks. Add back and see how you feel. If bothersome symptoms return, then you have your answer.

My favorite gluten-free flours are the Cup for Cup, Namaste, Bob's Red Mill 1:1 and my own special grain-free flour blend.

CHRONIC INFLAMMATION AND "THE LEAKY GUT"

For autoimmune conditions and other disorders related to inflammation, the concept of a "leaky gut", or increased intestinal permeability, has come into the conversation over the last few years. Alzheimer's disease, gingivitis, allergies, asthma, autoimmune diseases, cardiovascular disease, arthritis, metabolic syndrome and even cancers are profoundly influenced by inflammation. Where does this inflammation come from? How can we fix it?

It's a complex answer, including environmental pollutants, including plastics and pesticides, toxic stress and chronic activation of the sympathetic nervous system, but the number one influencer is at the end of our fork. The gut is the gateway for inflammation to enter the body and the food we eat makes a difference.

The small intestine is the part of the gastrointestinal tract where nutrients are absorbed. These cells in the intestine are linked together, one cell layer thick, with tight junctions. Right underneath that single-cell layer lies approximately 70% of the lymphoid (immune) cells in the body. When food, additives, sugars, and artificial sweeteners create inflammation in the intestine, swelling causes the tight junctions to become permeable. Permeability in the junctions exposes the underlying lymphoid tissue to a host of foreign material. This foreign material passes through the junction to lymphoid cells and is then carried into the bloodstream.

How does the body respond to this foreign material? An inflammatory cascade ensues, forming antibodies to "foreign" materials. The body can also respond by forming inappropriate self-antibodies – a proposed pathogenesis for autoimmune disease. This chronic inflammation in the gut is where treatment of autoimmune disease needs to start. If there is inflammation in the gut, there will be inflammation in the body, fanning the flames of diseases now affecting much of the American population. We literally get pounds of "information" on the end of our forks every day, profoundly affecting our gut health and overall well-being. What we eat matters.

All of the recipes in this book are designed to create or maintain a healthy gut. I am a believer that you cannot truly be healthy until the gut is well. The way to do that is through a conscious diet.

WHAT ABOUT PROBIOTICS?

One of the supplements I routinely recommend for patients is a high-quality probiotic. When I started my medical practice, probiotics were not routinely discussed and very little was known about the gut microbiome and its wide-reaching effects on overall health status. The conversation has changed. An abundance of research is focusing on the gut microbiome's effects on multiple disease processes, from mental health to autoimmune diseases to acne to obesity and more. As an OB/GYN, I often see the effects of microbiome dysbiosis on the urogenital tract and as it relates to maternal-child healthcare.

Here are my recommendations for optimizing the body's microbiome:

For urogenital and maternal-child health, Lactobacillus rhamnosus (GG) and Lactobacillus reuteri have the most data. L. rhamnosus is effective in preventing vaginal infections and as an adjuvant treatment therapy in recurrent, hard-to-treat infections and can prevent urinary tract infection and resolve diarrheal infections as well. I always supplement my pregnant patients with L. reuteri, especially at 36 weeks to delivery. Studies show that this probiotic, when given at the end of pregnancy and during breastfeeding, is effective at reducing the risk of atopic disease, eczema and allergies in the child.

For general gut health, I recommend a combination of Lactobacillus casei (especially important for people with autoimmune disease), saccharomyces and bifidobacterium.

Natural food sources of probiotics should also be consumed, such as unsweetened yogurt, sauerkraut, kimchi, kombucha (fermented tea) and pickled vegetables. For most Americans, their diet is not rich in natural probiotics and a supplement is advisable.

Prebiotics are an important part of my recipes and are the "food" that the probiotics digest and use to proliferate in the body. The "resistant" starches in legumes and sweet potatoes, for example, are used by the probiotics to replicate and repopulate the entire GI tract. A balanced diet will incorporate both prebiotic and probiotic foods to create a healthy microbiome.

DR. KENNARD'S KITCHENWARE

As you've probably guessed, I love to cook. I wanted quality cookware that was safe, and it had to be relatively affordable, since I bought it during medical school. While inexpensive, these pieces are healthy and durable.

Cast-iron skillet, seasoned
Cast-iron Dutch oven
Stainless steel cookware set, including a fry pan, a saucepan and a large stockpot (All-Clad is wonderful but expensive; I love my Kirkland brand set from Costco)
Wooden spoons
Silicone spatula
Stainless steel cooking utensils
Stainless steel steamer
Parchment paper to line baking sheets
Tempered glass storage containers
I do also love my Instant Pot, but this is not a necessity for any recipe in this book.

Please consider avoiding nonstick cookware; these often contain perfluorooctanoic acid (PFOA) and polytetrafluoroethylene (PTFE). These chemicals can leach during cooking and are even found in placental tissue and breast milk in studies. They are associated with dyslipidemia, cardiovascular risk, immune system dysfunction, developmental and neurological problems, and listed as a possible carcinogen. Nonstick coating is easily damaged with a utensil or during cleaning and will start to leach the chemical into the food. Reasonable non stick alternatives are ceramic cast-iron pans, seasoned cast iron (naturally non stick) or a stainless steel fry pan used with an oil that tolerates high-heat cooking like butter, coconut or avocado oil. Once you have eliminated anything with nonstick coating, you won't need a separate set of "soft" utensils to avoid damaging the pan. This is an added advantage.

Avoid baking or grilling on aluminum foil, as it can leach excess aluminum into the food. Parchment paper or silicone is a safer choice as it is heat stable to over 500 degrees.

When possible, please store food in glass or stainless-steel containers. Especially when the food is hot, the warmth can cause leaching of plastics from containers into food. Never heat food in plastic, even in BPA-free plastics, Other chemicals, some more toxic than BPA, can leach into food and have been implicated in early puberty, hormonal disorders and some cancers. Pyrex glass containers with lids work well and can go oven to table to dishwasher. For soups, I love using large mason jars that are inexpensive and readily available.

I am a fan of glass and stainless steel baby bottles for this reason as well, as plastics can break down in the dishwasher or when heating stored breast milk or formula. Babies have the highest rates of plastics in their system of all humans, with potentially concerning effects. Whenever possible, avoid plastics, both for personal health and for that of the planet.

FOOD AS MEDICINE

60-SECOND SIMPLE GREENS

This go-to salad allows the delicate flavor of the greens to be the highlight and is ready in less than one minute.

Begin with any organic greens. Choosing lettuce with deep green, purple or red hues increases the amount of phytonutrients available. Gradually add bitter greens such as arugula, kale, escarole and Swiss chard. The American diet is not used to bitter flavors, so add these vegetables gradually to accustom the palate. Bitter greens have been used for centuries to help stimulate secretion of gastric hydrochloric acid, improve digestion and are a natural way to prevent heartburn. In the typical American diet, greens are merely a vessel for unhealthy dressings and toppings, but in a medicinal and traditional sense, the salad greens provided vital nutrients, improved digestion and were served before the main meal.

Adding olive oil to greens not only adds potent anti-inflammatory unsaturated fatty acids, but also actually increases the absorption of the fat-soluble vitamins in the greens. A staple in the Mediterranean diet, Olive oil has withstood the test of time and science as one of the healthiest foods on the planet. Choose olive oil with a peppery bite at the back of the throat, which comes from a high polyphenol content. Cracked black pepper milled over the top of the salad further stimulates secretion of gastric juices, aiding in improved digestion. Any citrus will work well; I particularly enjoy the flavors of Meyer lemon and tangerine in this salad.

4 c organic fresh greens

Dressing:
¼ c extra virgin olive oil
4 T red wine vinegar
1 T citrus zest
Squeeze of citrus

Whisk dressing ingredients together and pour over greens. Toss and serve.

BRIGHT LIGHTS SALAD

An antioxidant burst! The bright colors of the rainbow chard stalks, pomegranates and deep green leaves are rich in polyphenols and antioxidants. The absorption of these nutrients is enhanced with the healthy fats from olive oil and walnuts. The bitter greens enhance digestion, acting as prebiotics to optimize a healthy microbiome.

2 c greens

1 c blueberries

2 c chopped rainbow chard

¼ c pomegranate seeds

¼ c chopped walnuts

Pomegranate vinaigrette:

½ c extra virgin olive oil

¼ c pomegranate juice

¼ c white wine vinegar

1 T orange zest

Pepper to taste

Mix the greens, pomegranate seeds, and walnuts together. In a separate bowl, whisk the dressing ingredients together. Toss and serve.

DR. K'S IMMUNE BOOST LENTIL STEW

I created this immune-boosting soup for a friend with cancer when he was undergoing chemotherapy. The mushrooms and astragalus impart a direct immunomodulatory effect, improving innate immunity when the system is down and even offering cancer-fighting properties to aid alongside the chemotherapy. The warming spices and alimental vegetables pack a further punch against common infections that we are all susceptible to during cold and flu season. The bone broth base is deeply nourishing and great for those with autoimmune issues as well.

1 leek, chopped
6 stalks of celery, chopped
1 shallot, chopped
2 T fresh turmeric root, grated or 1 T dried turmeric powder
2 t cinnamon
1 t cardamom
1 t cumin
1 t coriander
4 T avocado oil or ghee
1 c chopped medicinal mushrooms, such as shiitake or maitake
2 c chopped rainbow chard, separated into stems and leaves
2 c red lentils
6 c bone broth
Optional: 2 T chopped astragalus root

Sauté leek, celery, chard stalks and shallot in avocado oil or ghee to soften, along with spices to release aromatics. Add remainder of ingredients and cook covered until lentils are soft.

MEDICINAL SPOTLIGHT: ASTRAGALUS

Astragalus is a perennial herb revered in Traditional Chinese Medicine as an immune-strengthening tonic, augmenting the body's natural reserves and flow of energy (Qi). It is grown for two years and the roots are harvested. The root can also be purchased as a powder or cut root for simmering in a soup.

MEDICINAL MUSHROOMS: NATURE'S IMMUNE MODULATOR

You might notice that many of my recipes call for "medicinal mushrooms." What are these and why are they important?

Medicinal mushrooms are not the typical white button mushroom found on a salad bar or even the common Portobello and crimini mushrooms. These mushrooms actually have been shown to contain natural carcinogens, which degrades with high temperature cooking. Regardless, I would recommend avoiding those types and focusing on the many species that have strong anticancer and immunomodulatory benefits. The beneficial varietals include the more colorful, large and oddly-shaped species, including shiitake, maitake, turkey tail, reishi, cordyceps, chanterelle, lion's mane and enoki mushrooms.

Shiitake, maitake, chanterelle and enoki mushrooms are palatable and a good addition to culinary medicine recipes. They have anti-cancer effects, slowing tumor growth and boosting the immune system, improving the body's natural defenses. Maitake mushrooms, in particular, are powerful at modulating the immune response to be an appropriate, strong response without aggravating autoimmune conditions. For flavor, the yellow chanterelle mushroom is my favorite.

In a strictly medicinal role, reishi, turkey tail and lion's mane varietals shine. Reishi is bitter on its own but can be tolerated in teas or in capsules. Along with tumor fighting and immune modulating properties, reishi has an anti-inflammatory effect that I particularly like for folks struggling with autoimmune disorders. Lion's mane is believed to stimulate nerve growth and a small Japanese study showed cognitive improvement with lion's mane supplementation. Turkey tail mushrooms, which resemble a beautiful turkey tail in appearance, are another mushroom with proven anti-cancer effects.

Many of these mushrooms are commercially available in health food stores today and powders and teas are also starting to enter the marketplace. I think medicinal mushrooms are worth adding on a daily basis. In large meta-analysis studies on colon cancer survival, patients that were given turkey tail in addition to their chemotherapy had 29% increased survival and a 28% increased disease-free interval compared to those given standard chemotherapy alone, in a dose of 3 grams per day. Another pilot trial demonstrated an 88% clearance of a high-risk strain of human papillomavirus, compared to 5% clearance for the control group. Clearly, the turkey tail mushroom, or trametes versicolor, is immunologically active and beneficial.

SWEET POTATO & TURKEY CHILI

An extra vegetable boost adds nutritional value to this chili. The spices are enhanced by the smoked paprika, giving the chili a dimension of flavor and richness that is balanced by the sweetness of the sweet potato. Hearty, healthy, and filling!

1 lb. organic, pastured ground turkey
3 T avocado oil
1 can or bag BPA-free kidney beans
1 can or bag BPA-free white northern beans
1 jar or box of diced tomatoes
5 stalks celery, diced
1 diced sweet bell pepper
1 diced sweet onion
2 sweet potatoes, diced
2 T chili powder
1 T smoked paprika
Pinch cayenne pepper
Salt and pepper to taste
1 avocado, sliced
1 c grass-fed sharp cheddar, grated

Heat avocado oil in skillet. Add turkey, onion, celery and spices. Cook until turkey is browned, vegetables are soft and seasonings are fragrant. Add tomatoes, beans and remaining vegetables. Bring to a boil and simmer for 30 minutes. Serve topped with sliced avocado and grass-fed cheddar.

BONE BROTH

When my Traditional Chinese Medicine doctor suggested bone broth to me during my pregnancy, the concept was foreign. It hadn't hit the shelves yet in every form possible, as the newest trendy superfood to arrive at Whole Foods or in a subscription box. But the doctor's recommendation was sound; she had suggested it to me during pregnancy to build blood, support Qi and nourish the kidneys. Chinese Medicine traditionally has been empirical science, which means that they experimented and observed nature and continually confirmed their conclusions over time. Only recently have Western studies confirmed what that system has known for millennia. There is a reason the same practices have been passed down from generation to generation – they work! Bone broth is one of those examples; our culture has just learned about and accepted what ancient medicine has known.

Now there are many bone broth products that can easily be purchased, but they tend to be expensive with a lot of packaging. I make bone broth at home with minimal effort. It helps if you have an Instant Pot to speed up the timing, but stovetop will work just as well.

Start with one whole chicken, cooked. To expedite dinner, sometimes I will buy a pre-cooked rotisserie chicken from the market. These bones work just as well. Alternatively, you can cook a whole chicken at home yourself. Use the meat for dinner. Afterwards, return the bones (chicken or beef) to the pot and cover with enough water to completely cover them. Add 2 T apple cider vinegar. Add some herbs or vegetables for flavor. In chicken broth, I love savory flavors – thyme, rosemary, sage and scraps of celery, leek and carrot. In the beef broth, I prefer the warming bite of turmeric and ginger.

Simmer on the stovetop for 6-8 hours on low, in the crock-pot for 10-12 hours on low or in the Instant Pot for 2 hours on high manual pressure. Run the liquid through cheesecloth or a fine sieve to strain the broth.

You will see some fat (sometimes even a layer of fat) on the top of the broth when it is refrigerated. Do not get rid of this! This is the "good stuff"- the collagen which provides lubrication for the joints and healing to the gut mucosa. Just warm it up and the layer will dissipate into the protein-rich broth.

Bone broth is warm and healing when sipped on its own. It can be mixed into a soup, or I like to use it instead of water when cooking rice or quinoa for some extra nutrition.

BONE BROTH JASMINE RICE

This recipe is simply replacing the water in a typical rice recipe with bone broth. Bone broth is easy to make, especially with a modern-day pressure cooker. Its benefits are numerous, and it makes a plain grain more tasty and nutritious. It can be substituted one for one with water or other liquids when making rice, quinoa, lentils or any other grain.

To decrease the amount that the blood sugar will rise after eating a carbohydrate, called glycemic load, refrigerate the rice immediately after cooking and then reheat to serve.

2 cups of bone broth

1 cup jasmine rice

Boil bone broth and stir in rice. Reduce heat and simmer, covered, for 20 minutes, until the rice is soft.

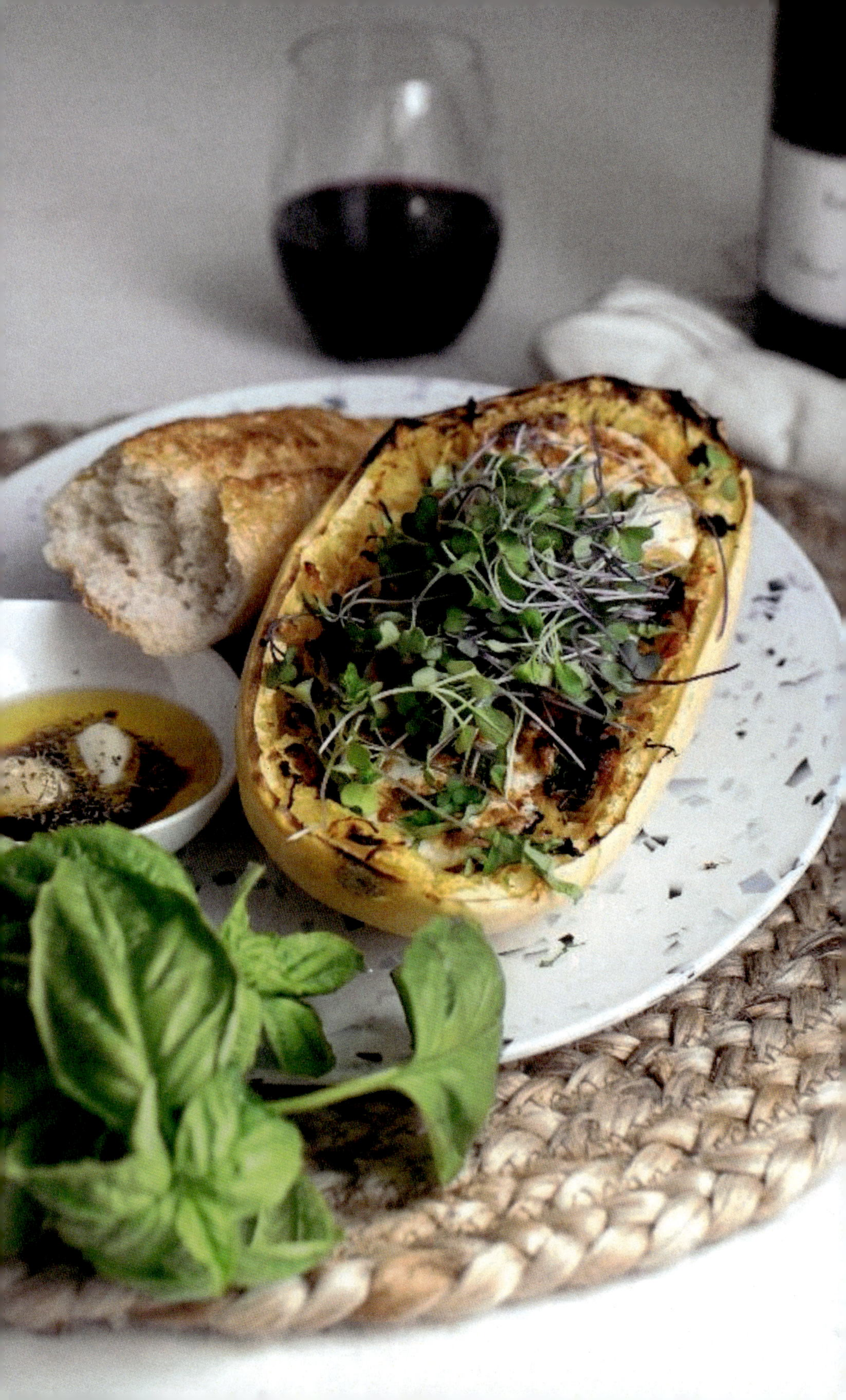

ROASTED SPAGHETTI SQUASH CASSEROLE

This recipe is so lovely, because it creates a low carbohydrate, high phytonutrient version of a delicious Italian recipe. This is a true medicinal recipe, between the antioxidants from the squash, kale, tomatoes and the immune supporting and cancer fighting properties of the medicinal mushrooms. The olive oil adds a powerful dose of polyunsaturated fats and is one of the most anti-inflammatory foods on the planet. It is a warming, delicious fall meal when spaghetti squash is in season.

One spaghetti squash
¼ c cold pressed, extra virgin olive oil
2 T fresh basil chopped
1 T oregano, dried or fresh, chopped
2 tsp. marjoram, chopped
14 oz BPA-free can or jar of diced tomatoes, I prefer fire roasted

3 leaves of dinosaur kale, de-ribbed and chopped

1 c chopped medicinal mushrooms

Optional: 1 cup nitrate free sausage, chopped into bite-sized pieces

Baste the spaghetti squash with olive oil and place in a pan. Roast the spaghetti squash at 425° for 20 minutes. Remove the squash from oven. Shred spaghetti squash into a large bowl, reserving the skins. Mix the mushrooms, tomatoes, kale, herbs and optional meat in with the spaghetti squash. Place the spaghetti squash mix back into the skin. Top with parmesan cheese. Roast in the oven for 25 minutes until the cheese bubbles.

FALL HARVEST ROASTED SQUASH

This dish has all the glory of the fall harvest. Any hard squash will work; I prefer the acorn and delicata varietals. This warm fall dish offers the peak nutrition of the potent phytonutrients of the chard and apple, the anti-cancer and immune boosting properties of the mushrooms and alimental vegetables and a strong dose of Vitamins A and C from the apple, squash and chard. The herbs for seasoning are also medicinal; the thyme, oregano, and rosemary are all potent antiseptics. No wonder these foods are seasonal to the fall, with their immune-boosting properties, just in time for the cold and flu season.

4 halved and hollowed hard squashes
1 lb. ground turkey, chicken thighs or turkey sausage (optional)
1 leek, chopped
1 shallot, chopped
1 onion, chopped
5 leaves rainbow chard, divided into leaves and stems
1 c medicinal mushrooms
1 chopped crisp apple; I like Honeycrisp, Braeburn or Pink Lady
2 c red lentil, cooked in bone broth when possible
2 carrots, chopped
1 parsnip, chopped
1 T thyme
1 tsp rosemary
1 T sage
1 tsp. oregano
½ c grated Manchego cheese

Drizzle the squash with olive oil on a baking pan and top with salt and pepper. Roast the squash in the oven at 425 for approximately 30 minutes.

Cook the lentils according to package directions, replacing water with bone broth for extra protein and gut health benefits.

Sauté the leek, onion, shallot, celery, chopped stems of the chard and all herbs in olive oil until soft. Add in the meat, if desired, cooking until browned. Add chopped carrots and parsnips, mushrooms and apple. When softened, add in the lentils and stir to make a thick filling for the squash. While the filling is hot, add the chopped chard leaves – they will naturally wilt without additional cook time.

Spoon the filling into the squash and top with grated manchego cheese. Place back into the oven until the cheese bubbles.

This filling can be mixed with bone broth for a wonderful fall soup that has all of the benefits of the ingredients above with the protein and collagen from bone broth.

MOROCCAN CHICKEN TAGINE

This North African style tagine is loaded with warm, filling flavors and powerful anti-inflammatory spices. It's one of my favorite one-pot Dutch oven meals. It also lends itself well to crock pot and pressure-cooking to be ready after a long day of work.

1 lb. boneless skinless Chicken thighs

1 sweet onion, chopped

2 T grated fresh Turmeric or 1 T dried

2 tsp. smoked Paprika

1 tsp. cumin

Pinch of cayenne pepper

2 tsp. grated fresh ginger or 1 tsp dried

1 tsp. cinnamon

1 tsp. coriander

2 T honey

1 T lemon zest or preserved lemon

Squeeze of Lemon juice

2 c kabocha squash, cubed

1 c bone broth

Heat oil in Dutch oven. Add onion, chicken thighs and seasonings until brown and spices are fragrant. Add honey and lemon zest and juice. Add bone broth. Prepare the squash by cutting in half and removing seeds. Cut into one-inch thick wedges. Using a vegetable peeler, remove some but not all of the skin. Cut wedges into small chunks. Stir in the squash and simmer, covered, for 45 minutes until squash is soft and flavors have blended.

Serve with bone broth rice.

GRATEFUL PIZZA

I call this the Grateful pizza because the ingredients are seasonal to autumn, the season of gratitude. Food should be joyful and so is this dish. There is so much nutrition, color and flavor in this pizza and it can be served all day. It is a wonderful brunch dish or unique enough to serve for a dinner party. The butternut squash in the crust adds a healthy dose of beta-carotene, along with fiber, potassium and vitamin B6. The above vegetables are just a suggestion; this can be made with just about anything. Broccoli rabe, asparagus, beets and summer squash are all wonderful additions to this pizza. In this recipe, the bitter greens balance the natural sweetness of the squash, with a pop of tartness from the antioxidant-rich pomegranate.

Gluten-free Butternut Squash Crust (Life hack: make a few extra and freeze them for later use)
1 c grated aged Italian cheeses
1 heirloom tomato, sliced

1 delicata squash

2 c chopped bitter greens (beet greens, escarole, radicchio, kale or chard)

1 pomegranate, seeded

1 tsp each thyme and marjoram

For the crust:

1 medium butternut squash or one can of squash

4 T extra virgin olive oil

1 egg

1 c gluten-free flour

½ c cornmeal

½ tsp. sea salt

Heat the oven to 425 degrees. Cut butternut squash lengthwise and scoop out seeds. Lay in roasting pan and brush with olive oil. After about 40 minutes, when soft, remove, cool and scoop out the flesh and puree.

Combine butternut puree with the remainder of the ingredients. Spread onto parchment or a pizza stone and bake for 20-25 minutes.

Note: these store well in the freezer. Make a large batch and then have the crust ready for a 10-minute pizza meal on a busy night.

Making the Pizza:

Halve delicata squash lengthwise. Scoop out seeds. Cut in ¼ inch rings. Place the delicata squash rings in a separate dish and brush with olive oil. Roast for about 15 minutes while preparing the pizza.

Brush the prepared crust with olive oil. Lay sliced heirloom tomatoes on the crust, top the tomato with the herbs and sprinkle lightly with Italian cheeses. Place the delicata rings on top and crack an egg into each ring; 2-3 per pizza.

Bake for 10 minutes.

Remove pizza and squash from oven. Top with chopped bitter greens and pomegranate seeds.

Of note, this pairs spectacularly well with an oaky chardonnay or Pinot Noir wine.

MEDICINAL SPOTLIGHT: BITTER GREENS

Escarole, chard, radicchio, and kale are all hardy greens that are forgiving to grow. Generally they prefer cooler weather, and are a hardy fall and spring crop for most North American climate zones. They will tolerate intermittent watering a few times per week. A particularly easy varietal to grow is lacinto, or dinosaur kale, which is particularly high in cancer-fighting phytonutrients, and is mild enough to eat raw in a salad.

SCARBOROUGH FAIR MEATBALLS

> *"Are you going to Scarborough Fair?*
> *Parsley, sage, rosemary and thyme*
> *Remember me to one who lives there*
> *For once she was a true love of mine."*
> —Simon and Garfunkel

My Scarborough Fair meatballs have all the herbs Simon and Garfunkel sang about, creating a homey, delicious meatball with plenty of herbal medicine on board via the flavonoids in parsley, thyme, rosemary, and sage.

1 lb. ground grass-fed beef

1 egg

½ c rolled gluten-free oats

½ c milk or almond milk

1 diced sweet onion

2 T chopped or ground sage

2 T chopped parsley

1 T chopped thyme

1 tsp. chopped rosemary

Pinch of salt

Pepper to taste

Combine all ingredients. Shape into meatballs and bake at 375 degrees for 25-30 minutes.

WHY GRASS-FED AND FINISHED BEEF?

My recipes specify use of grass-fed and finished beef. How is this different than commercial beef sold in most markets? Typically, cattle are fed mostly grain and corn. This changes the nutritional profile of their meat to have more inflammatory omega-6 fats as compared to anti-inflammatory omega-3 fats. A conventionally raised cow has a ratio of 20-40:1 omega 6 to omega 3. A cow that grazed on grass during its life has a much more favorable ratio of about 6:1 omega 6 to omega 3. If a conventional cow is labeled as "organic", that means that the corn feed was organic and does not denote any functional change in the nutritional value.

Even though the meat might look identical, grass-fed and grain-fed cows are completely different foods, and different information for the function of the body's cellular activities.

COCONUT CHICKEN AND VEGETABLE CURRY

This is a delightful anti-inflammatory curry. Turmeric lends the powerful antioxidant curcumin, healing to the gut and anti-inflammatory to the whole body when absorbed in the gut lining with black pepper. Coconut offers medium chain triglyceride forms of fat, good for cognition, satiety, and blood sugar stability. A rainbow of vegetables adds an array of antioxidants.

1 lb. boneless skinless chicken thighs

4 T coconut oil

1 can full fat coconut cream

2 heads bok choy, chopped

1 sweet bell pepper, chopped

2 carrots, chopped

2 medium sweet potatoes, chopped

1 c sugar snap peas, stems removed

4 leaves rainbow chard, chopped

2 T curry powder

2 T grated turmeric root

1 T grated ginger root

Black pepper to taste

Heat coconut oil in a wok or skillet. Add seasonings along with the chicken to brown and activate the flavor in the spices. Once browned, add in the coconut cream and all of the vegetables, except the bok choy and chard leaves. Bring to a boil and then simmer for 30 minutes until the vegetables soften. Add the bok choy and chard leaves and simmer for another 10 minutes until the leaves are soft and brightly colored. Remove the chicken, chop and return. Serve over bone broth jasmine rice.

Instant Pot Cook Instructions:

Heat coconut oil in sauté mode, adding chicken and spices. Brown chicken and aliven spices. Add all vegetables to pot with coconut cream and cook on high, manual mode, for 11 minutes. Natural release for 10 minutes. Chop chicken and return to pot. Serve.

SWEET POTATO EGG SKILLET

This is a beautiful dish for any time of day and is my go-to when I'm hosting a brunch. Full of protein, phytonutrients, fiber, prebiotics, choline and healthy fat, it's a solid staple as a main dish. Choline is a nutrient that was deficient in the American diet as eggs became a villain in the low-fat decades. Cook and serve in a cast iron skillet if possible, for the best caramelization, heat retention and a little extra iron in your dish.

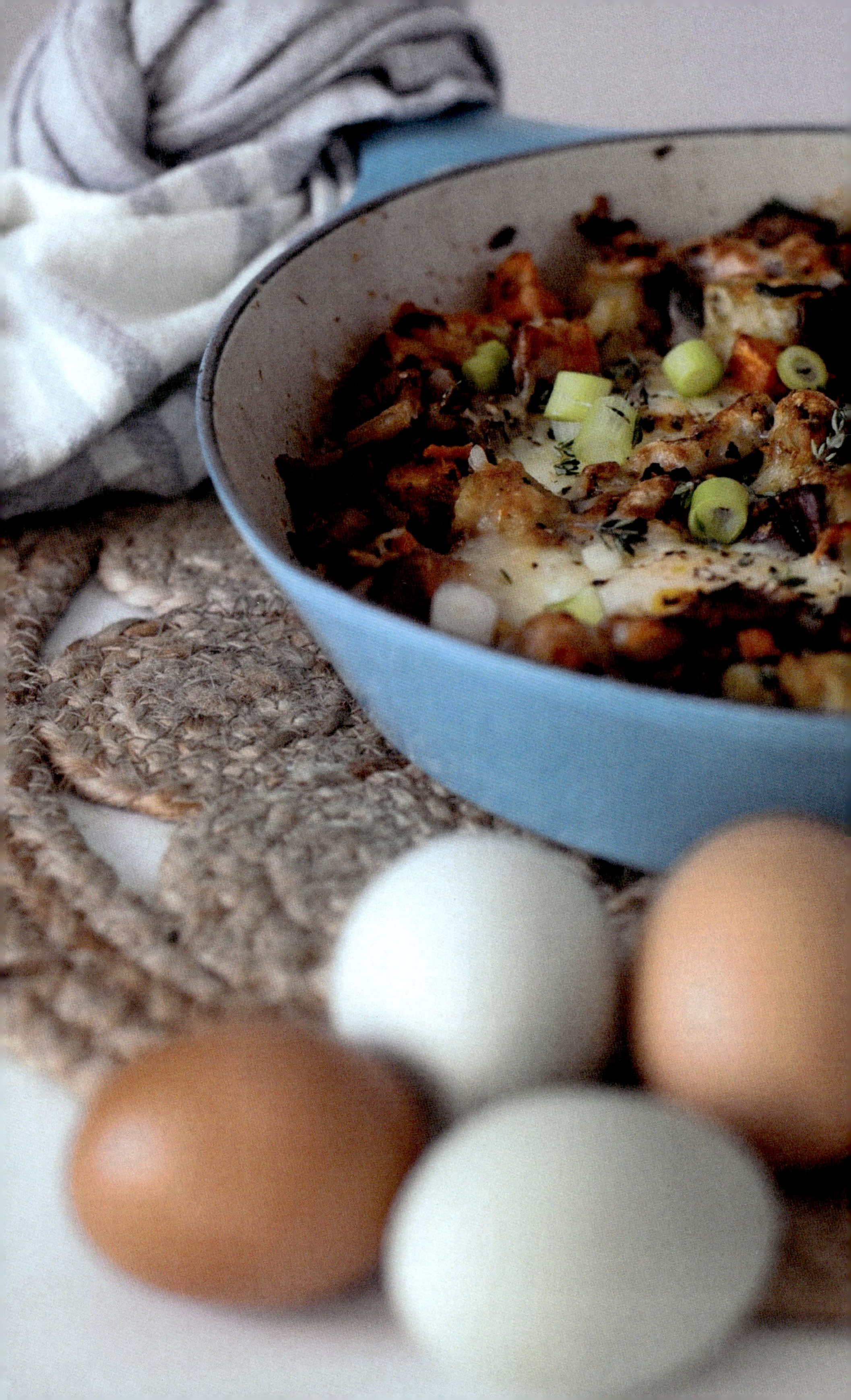

3 T avocado oil

6 sweet potatoes of any varietal (yellow, orange or purple)

1 small sweet onion

4-5 rainbow chard leaves

6 pastured eggs

Optional: 1 c nitrite free chopped, cooked bacon (I like Applegate Farms brand)

Salt and pepper to taste

Chopped scallions

1 avocado, sliced

Heat cast iron skillet with avocado oil. Add diced sweet potato and onion and cook until caramelized and softened. Add rainbow chard and sauté for another 3-4 min until softened. Add bacon, if desired. Dig 6 wells in the sweet potato mixture and crack an egg into each. Place into oven at 400 degrees for 8 minutes, until egg is firm to touch, but yolk is not fully cooked. Remove and top with scallions. Serve with sliced avocado.

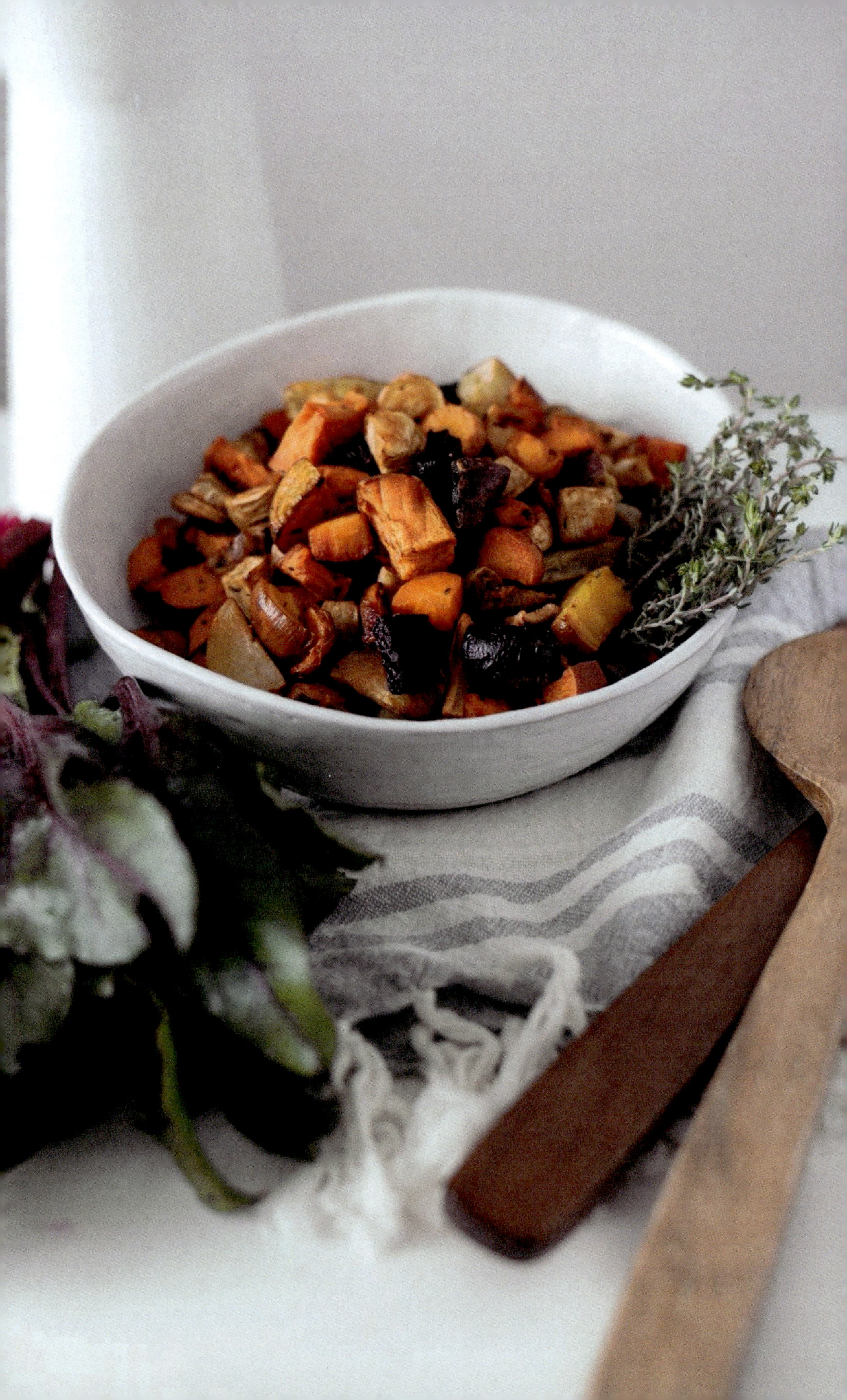

ROASTED ROOT VEGGIES

Garnet, yam, yellow sweet potatoes and purple sweet potatoes are all excellent choices in this recipe. I prefer to use a couple different varietals at a time to maximize the different nutritional benefits. Carotenoids, flavonoids, Vitamins A and C, healthy fat and germ-fighting seasoning…this is a great side dish to a holiday meal or base for a Buddha bowl.

2 parsnips, sliced
3-4 sweet potatoes, cubed
3 beets, golden or red, cubed
3 carrots, sliced
¼ c extra virgin olive oil
2 tsp. thyme
2 tsp. parsley
Salt and pepper to taste

Mix all vegetables in a bowl with olive oil. Add spices. Spread on baking sheet and bake at 400 degrees for 35-45 minutes, tossing vegetables twice during cooking time for even caramelization and flavor.

ROOT VEGGIE BUDDHA BOWL

This is a make-ahead lunch for workday fuel! Full of filling healthy fats, fiber and an array of inflammation-fighting phytonutrients, this is a dish that keeps well in the refrigerator and can be prepared up to three days ahead of time. Add some extra love for the gut by using bone broth while preparing the quinoa.

1 c roasted root veggies
½ c bone broth quinoa
1 avocado
1 c greens
2 T olive oil
Squeeze of lemon

Warm the quinoa and root veggies if desired. Top with remaining ingredients.

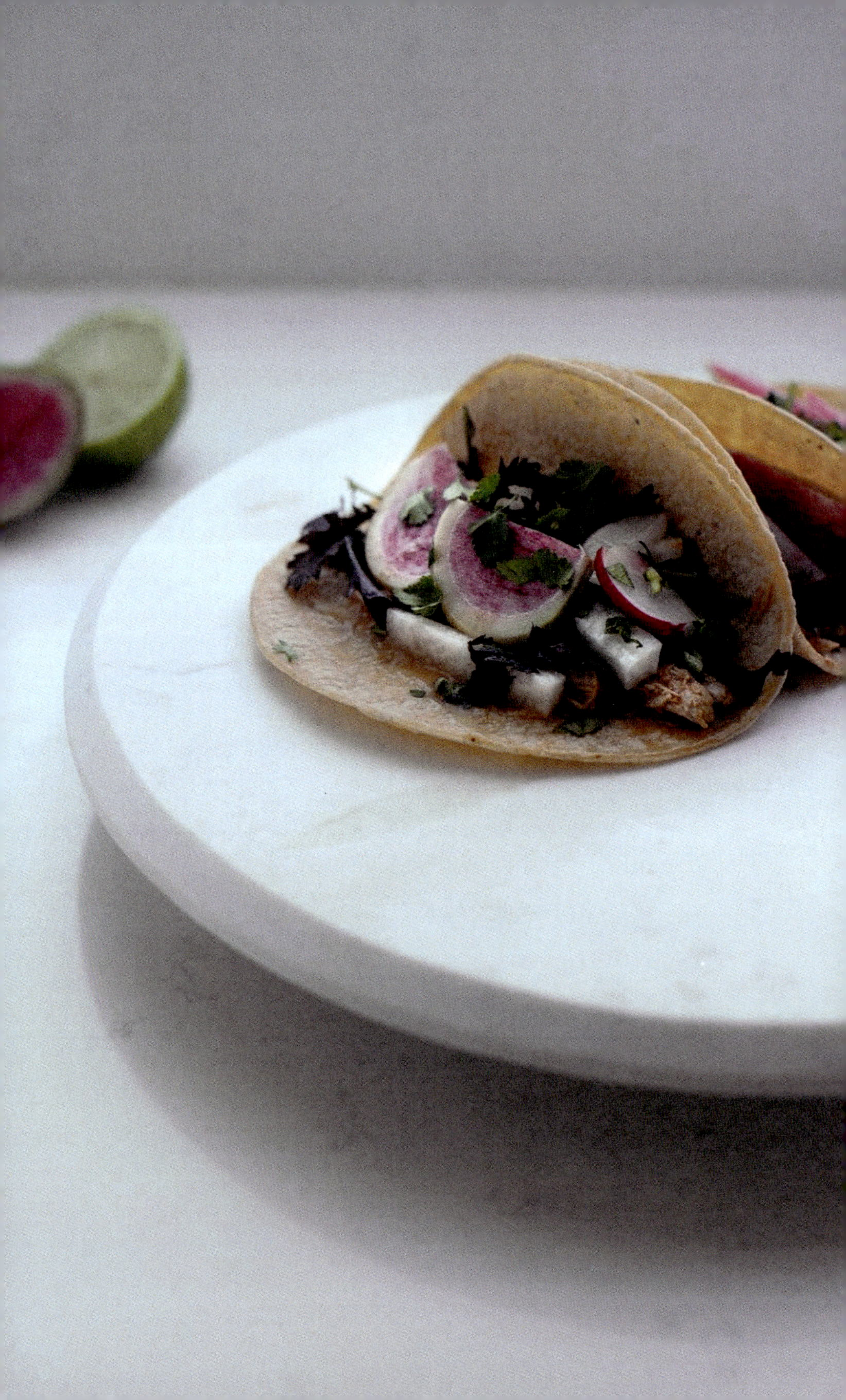

WATERMELON CHICKEN TACOS

Daikon, or watermelon radish, is a type of cruciferous vegetable high in several types of carotenoids, along with vitamins and minerals. When cut open, it has a delightful "watermelon" type appearance with rich pink outlined by a light green rind. This is accompanied by sweet watermelon, jicama, red cabbage, cilantro, and lime for a polyphenol rich slaw atop pulled chicken. This is always a hit for a summer meal, and an easy one to come home to after a long day of work, thanks to the slow cooked chicken!

Ingredients:
1 lb boneless, skinless, pasture raised chicken thighs or breasts
½ jar naturally sweetened BBQ sauce; I like Whole Foods' brand
¼ tsp each cumin, smoked paprika
A pinch of cayenne pepper, if desired

1 daikon radish, halved and sliced

1 c peeled and diced watermelon

1 c jicama, peeled and diced

1 c red cabbage, chopped

2 T chopped cilantro

¼ c white wine vinegar

½ c extra virgin olive oil

Corn, coconut flour, or cassava flour tortillas

Combine the chicken, BBQ sauce, and spices in a slow cooker. Cook on low for 8 hours. Alternately, this can be cooked in an Instant Pot on high manual for 15 minutes. Shred chicken using two forks or by mixing in a stand mixer with the standard paddle.

Combine all vegetables, oil, and vinegar.

Top tortillas with chicken and slaw. Enjoy!

DR. K'S GRAIN-FREE FLOUR BLEND

This is what I use for grain-free baking. It mimics the texture and flavor of regular flour and can be used in a one to one substitution for wheat flour. Using this should be a consideration in patients that have disorders of inflammation, particularly autoimmune diseases.

1 c almond flour
1 c cassava flour
½ c coconut flour

Use cup for cup in place of flour in any recipe.

PISTACHIO PUMPKIN APPLE MUFFINS

These muffins are healthy enough, without any added sugar, that I will happily let my preschooler eat them! They are a wonderful snack with some almond butter and a hot herbal tea. They are naturally sweetened by the applesauce. Some honey may be added for additional sweetness if desired. The cinnamon is a natural lowering agent for blood sugar and the fat from the butter balances the carbohydrate of the flour and oats, providing stable blood sugar and satiety. The warming spices add a wonderful fall flavor to this seasonal pastry.

1 can of pumpkin or other pureed squash (Acorn, Delicata and Butternut all work well)

½ c applesauce, no sugar added

2 eggs

1 tsp. vanilla extract

1 stick grass-fed butter, softened

¼ c raw honey

1 tsp. baking powder

½ tsp. baking soda

2 c gluten-free flour or Dr. K's Grain-Free flour blend

1 c gluten-free rolled oats

¼ tsp each of warming spices- cinnamon, nutmeg, cardamom, ginger

½ C chopped pistachio

Preheat oven to 375. Whip the butter, adding in the other wet ingredients. Add the warming spices, baking powder and baking soda. Add in the flour and oats last. Do not overmix. Place in muffin tins. Top with chopped pistachio. Bake for 15-18 minutes

Makes 24 muffins

Serve warm with grass-fed butter and raw honey.

DR. K'S HERBAL POWERBALLS

This is one of my favorite recipes because it is so easy to combine good food and herbal medicine. These powerballs are an easy breakfast or after school snack and provide a full dose of medicine in each serving. They can be customized by using different add-ins, like flaked coconut, dried fruit, and dark chocolate chips, and rolled in oats, cacao, or chia seeds. The protein and healthy fats in this recipe lower the glycemic index and provide long lasting energy and satiety.

BASIC POWERBALL RECIPE

1 C rolled oats
½ C ground flax
1 C natural almond butter
1/2 C raw honey

TUMMY LOVE POWERBALLS

This is such a great recipe for anyone needing a little extra love in the gut. triphala is an Ayurvedic combination of three astringent fruits that increase intestinal motility and normalize the gut microbiome. The probiotics add an extra dose of love for the gut, along with the Ayurvedic warming spices, fiber from oats and flax, and prebiotics from coconut.

Prepare the basic recipe and add:

2 tsp probiotic powder (or open 5 probiotic capsules and pour the powder inside out; discard the capsules)
1 T triphala powder
¼ c flaked coconut
1 tsp cinnamon
1 tsp cardamom
½ c rolled oats

Mix all ingredients together, reserving the oats in a bowl. Roll into balls in the bowl to coat the Powerballs with oats. Store in airtight container in the refrigerator.

CACAO IMMUNITY POWERBALLS

This is in my fridge all winter! Reishi mushroom is an immunomodulator, optimizing immune cell function, along with astragalus. Dark chocolate chips and cacao add a polyphenol boost, along with antioxidants from the cranberries.

Prepare the basic recipe and add:

2 tsp reishi mushroom powder
2 tsp astragalus powder
¼ c dried cranberries
½ c dark chocolate chips
½ c cacao powder

Combine all ingredients, reserving the cacoa in a bowl. Roll the balls in the cacao to coat the Powerballs. Store in airtight container in the refrigerator.

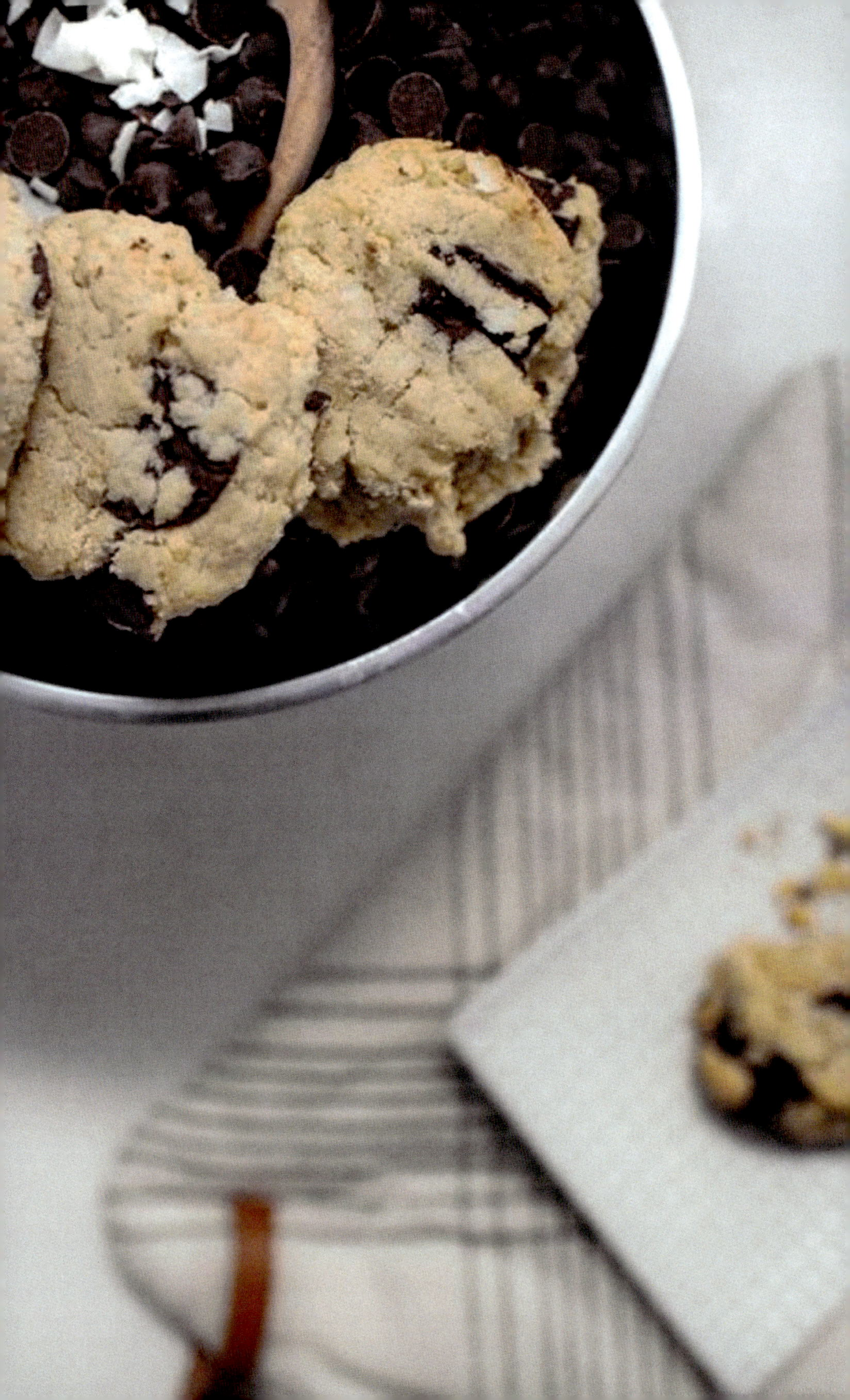

PALEO DARK CHOCOLATE, COCONUT AND SEA SALT COOKIES

A delicious option for a sweet treat! These cookies are chewy, delicious, and offer healthy fatty acids, grain-free low-glycemic index carbohydrate, and flavonoids from dark cacoa. Enjoy with a cup of adaptogen tea or homemade oat milk.

1 cup grass-fed butter

½ c granulated coconut sugar

2 eggs

2 tsp. vanilla extract

1 tsp. baking soda

2 ½ c Dr. K's grain-free flour blend

1 c dark chocolate chips (70% cacao or greater)

1 c unsweetened coconut flakes

Sea salt flakes

Beat the butter and sugar. Add vanilla and eggs and baking soda. Slowly add in the flour blend. Once fully mixed, add in the chocolate chips and coconut. Roll into balls and slightly flatten on a cookie sheet, sprinkling the top with sea salt flakes. Bake at 375 for 8-10 minutes.

BIG SUR GRANOLA

Big Sur is my favorite place to camp. The ocean, the redwoods, the natural hot springs, waterfalls and hiking creates a vacation that deeply connects to the Earth and the Self. I take along this granola for breakfast to go with a cup of camping coffee and another handful along for a hike. The fiber and healthy fats are filling and the mild coconut flavor along with the warming spices is lovely.

4 c rolled oats

1/4 c flax seeds

1 c whole roasted almonds

1 c roasted pistachios

1 T cinnamon

1 tsp. nutmeg

1 tsp. sea salt

3/4 c honey

½ c coconut oil

2 T vanilla

Combine the dry ingredients and set aside. Gently heat the honey, oil and vanilla until combined, then pour over dry ingredients and mix well. Spread in a greased baking sheet and bake at 325 degrees for 50 minutes, until the granola turns golden brown.

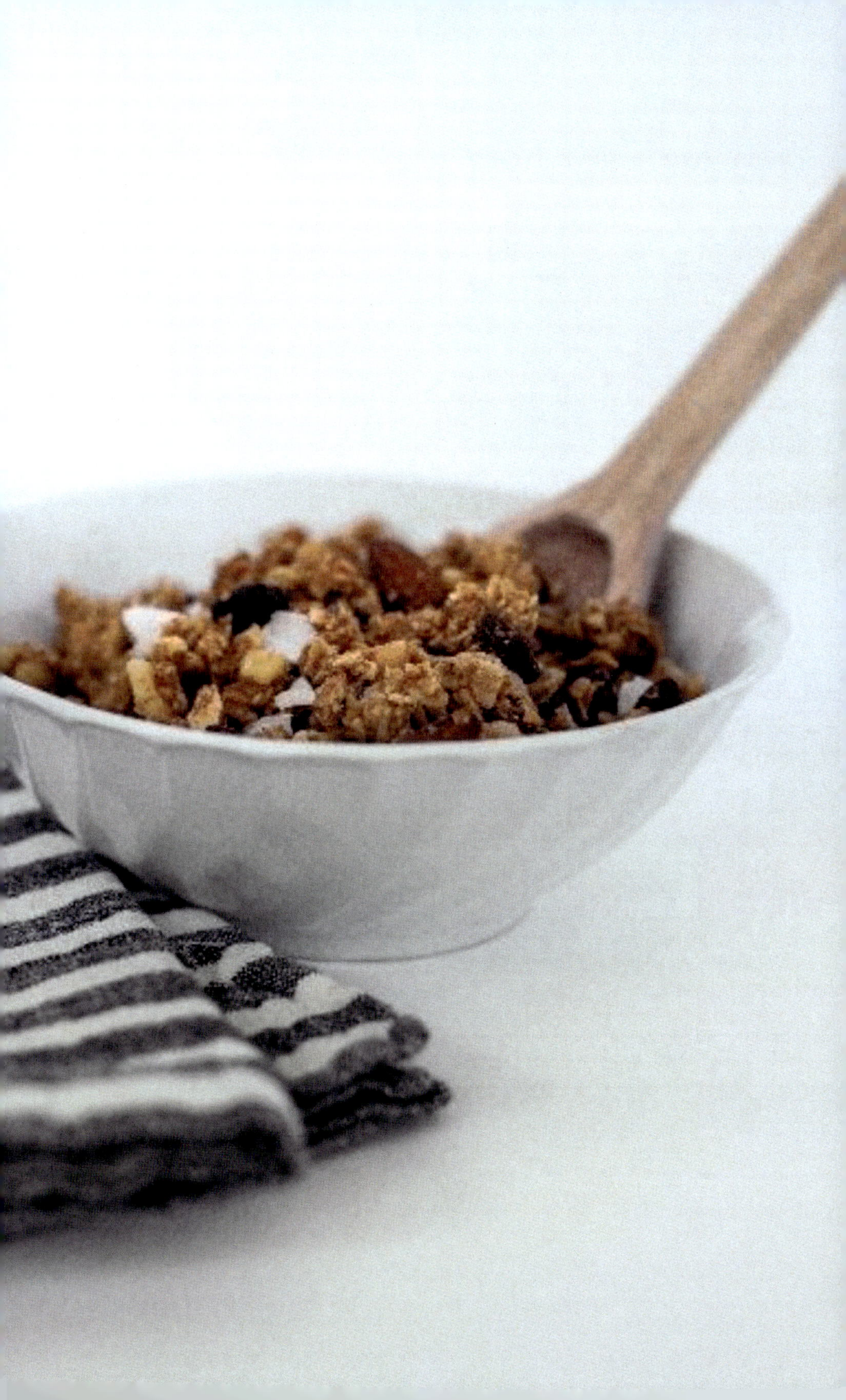

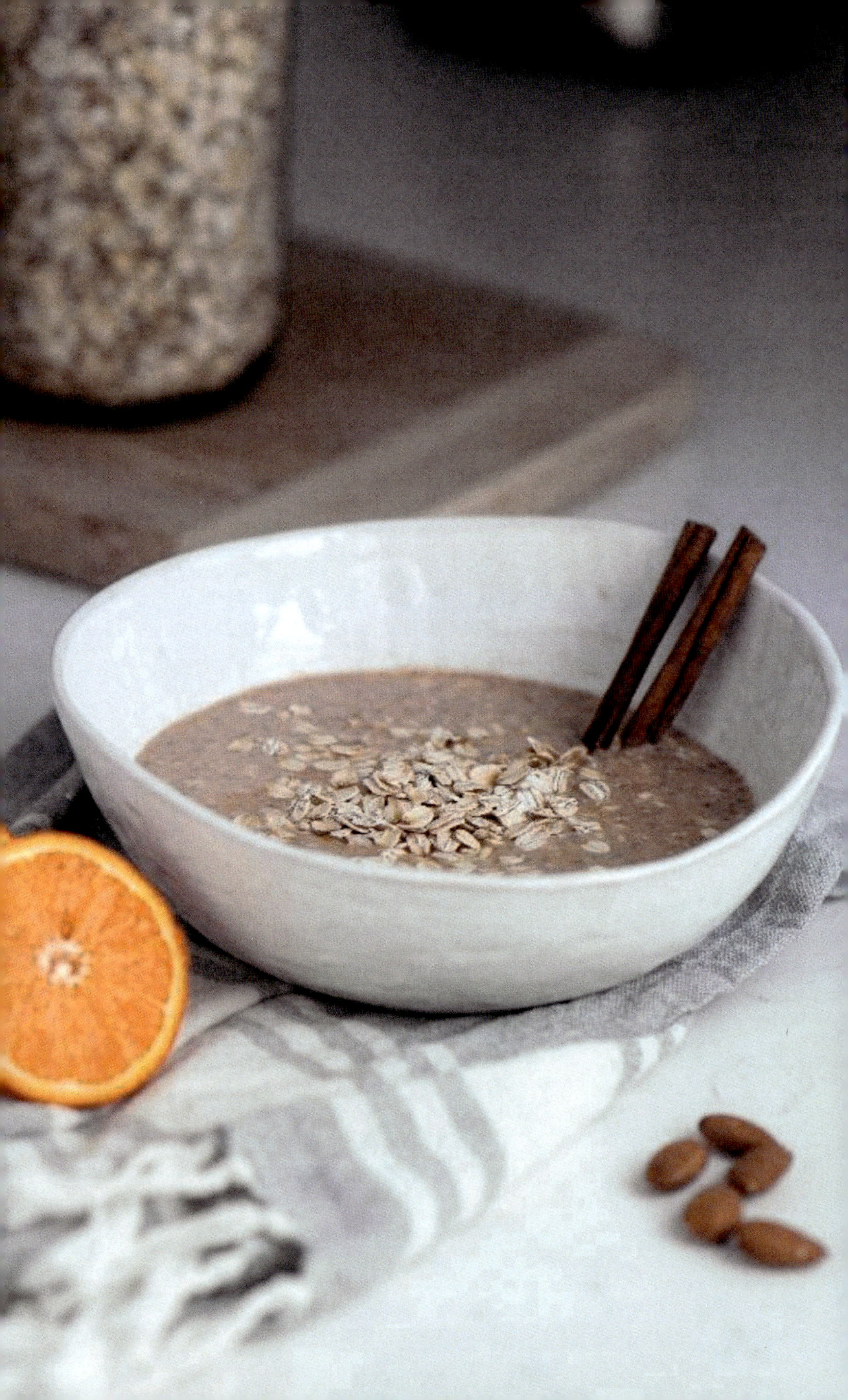

OVERNIGHT OATS AND CHIA PARFAIT

This breakfast is full of fiber, good fat and protein. It's a healthy grab and go option for busy folks who want to start the day off right.

1 quart mason jar
½ c gluten-free rolled oats
1 T raw honey
¼ c chia seeds
2 T ground flax
¼ c almond butter
1 c almond milk
1-2 tsp. warming spices, to taste (I like cinnamon, nutmeg, cardamom, ginger)

Place all ingredients in a mason jar and refrigerate overnight. In the morning, stir and go!

MEDICINAL SIPS

"TIRED AND WIRED" TEA

1 tsp Ashwagandha

2 tsp Tulsi

2 tsp lemon balm

Brew herbs in 16 oz of hot water for ten minutes

This lovely tea is for the "tired and wired" folks out there that need some help getting the nervous system to settle down. Ashwagandha and Tulsi are Ayurvedic adaptogens, modulating stress hormone production and providing a calming effect. The lemon balm is a lovely lemon-y flavored antidote for anxiety. It makes for a calming cup in the evening to wind down.

MEDICINAL GARDENING SPOTLIGHT: LEMON BALM (MELISSA OFFICINALIS)

Lemon balm, a member of the mint family, has been revered for centuries. It had a place in monastery gardens and was the one herb Charlemagne requested be planted in his garden, with good reason. Lemon balm relieves anxiety, decreases heartburn and gastrointestinal spasticity and has a lovely mild lemon taste. It can be brewed as a tea by soaking the leaves directly in water, either hot or as a tepid sun tea. It exhibits prolific growth and should be grown in a container unless spread is desired. Plant in partial shade, in moist soil. It can also be grown in a container on a windowsill. This is a must-have herb in your home.

MEDICINAL SPOTLIGHT: TULSI (OCIMUM SANCTUM

Tulsi, or holy basil, has been used in Ayurvedic medicine for thousands of years to promote health and well being. Modern research has affirmed this herb as an adaptogen, helping the body adapt to stress. Tulsi reduces oxidative stress, normalizes the stress response by decreasing cortisol, improves mood, and acts as an anti inflammatory. There are several delicious Tulsi teas on the market, or the herb can be used in cooking. Ancient wisdom for modern healing of 21st Century stress!

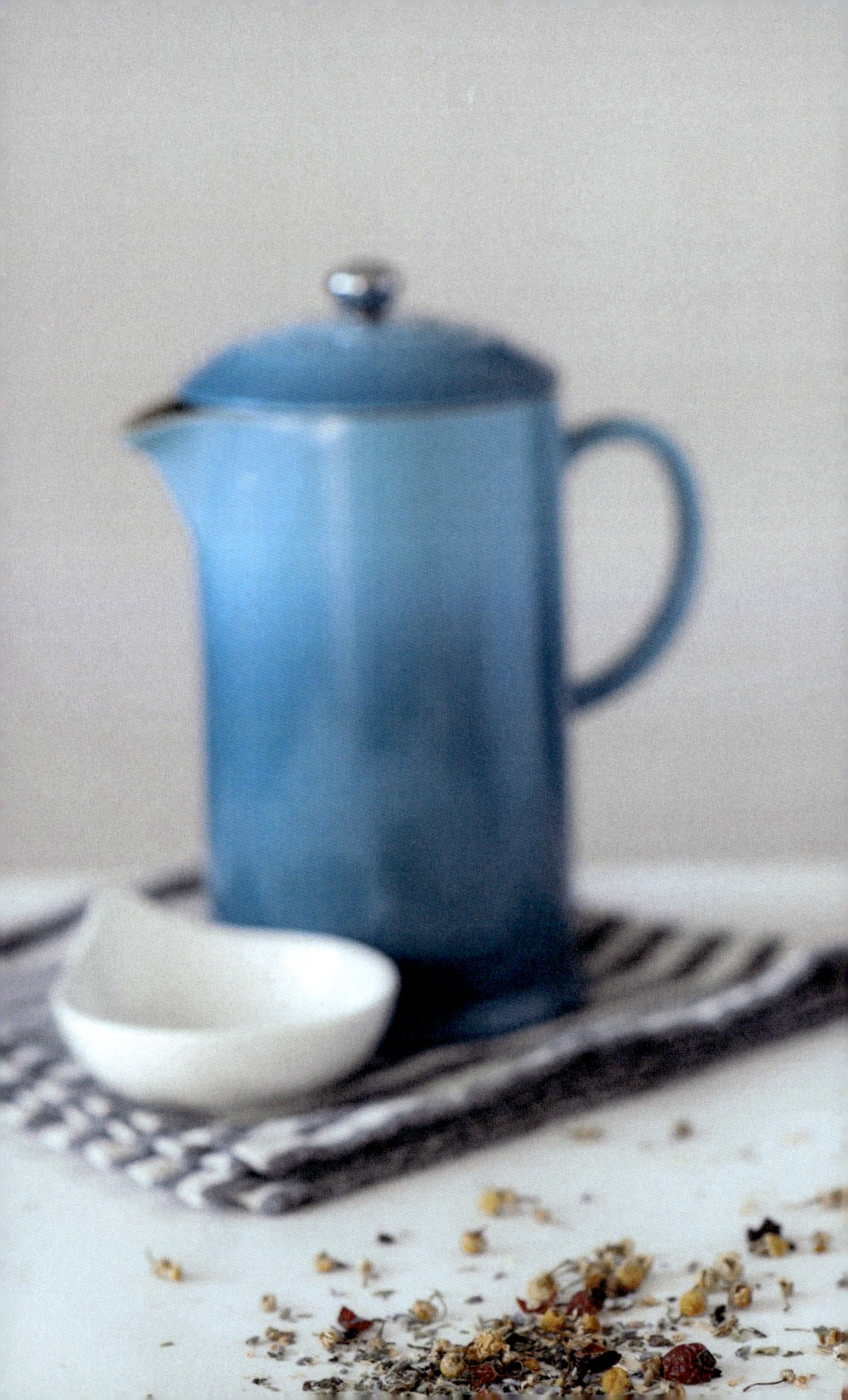

GINGER TEA

Ancient medicine for modern times, ginger has been used historically in Traditional Chinese Medicine and Ayurveda for millenia. Modern studies have affirmed ginger's ability to improve digestion, improve joint pain, decrease common cold symptoms, and even decrease menstrual cramping. In studies, one gram of dried ginger was equivalent to ibuprofen in relief of joint pain and menstrual cramping, by preventing the release of arachidonic acid and the subsequent breakdown to inflammatory leukotrienes and prostaglandins. In addition, one gram of ginger has been shown to significantly decrease nausea from both chemotherapy and pregnancy. Simple, but powerful, medicine in a cup!

2 T grated ginger root
8 oz water
Bring ginger and water to a boil and then simmer for 10 minutes. Serve with honey if desired.

HOT FLASH SUN TEA

Sage, usually thought of as a savory herb used around Thanksgiving time, is a cooling herb that works remarkably well for immediately improving menopausal hot flashes. I personally like this tea mixed with spearmint, for additional cooling and good flavor. Both herbs are readily available and easy to grow.

4 T sage leaves, coarsely chopped
2 T spearmint leaves, coarsely chopped

Place herbs in one quart of water. Leave in a sunny location for at least 24 hours. Refrigerate and drink iced.

MEDICINAL GARDENING SPOTLIGHT: SPEARMINT

Spearmint, a member of the mint family, will spread unchecked so it is best to grow this in a container. It is a hardy perennial that will tolerate a range of temperatures and partial shade to sunny conditions. It will also grow nicely on a windowsill. Pick the stems and pull off the leaves to use in the tea.

BEST REST TEA

I love herbs for helping to wind down and go to sleep at night. Good sleep practices are so important. I advise my patients to limit electronics two hours before bed, use a blue light filter on electronics in the evenings, schedule predictable sleep and wake times and utilize a calming and predictable routine to get ready for bed. Herbal tea is a nice addition to the evening routine; it is safe and effective for improving the ability to fall asleep and maintain restful sleep throughout the night. The chamomile and lemon balm are gentle relievers of anxiety, passionflower and valerian have a mild sedative property that helps people fall asleep and the hops improves the ability to stay soundly asleep overnight. Of note, valerian should be taken at least 14 days to determine efficacy.

1/3 c chamomile

1/3 c Lemon Balm

2 T Hops

2 T Passionflower

1 tsp. Valerian

Combine all herbs in a mason jar. Brew 2 T of loose-leaf tea for 10 minutes and enjoy.

MEDICINAL GARDENING SPOTLIGHT: CHAMOMILE

Chamomile is a hardy flowering plant that will grow well in partial shade to full sun, in a pot or in the ground. It is a workhorse to have in your garden, with uses ranging from relaxation, to the treatment of diarrhea, to soothing skin conditions. The flowers can be brewed in hot water as a tea or infused in oil to make a medicated salve.

HONEY "LEMON-AID"

Lemon balm and lavender add delightful delicate flavors and calming medicine to this "lemon-aid." Honey is a natural sweetener; use local and raw honey when possible for the most health benefits.

Honey Simple Syrup:
1 c honey
1 c water

Lemon-Aid:
1 c lemon juice (I prefer Meyer lemons)
6 c water
1 c honey simple syrup
1 sprig fresh lavender
4-5 sprigs fresh lemon balm

Bring a cup of water to a boil. Add honey until dissolved to make a simple syrup.

When cooled, add the lemon juice, water and herbs. Allow the herbs to steep for at least two hours. Strain out herbs and serve.

> ## MEDICINAL GARDENING SPOTLIGHT: LAVENDER
>
> **Lavender is a beautiful, drought tolerant plant that will grow in many climates with little care. Choose a full sun location with well-drained soil. It can be grown in the ground or in a pot. There are several varietals. I prefer the English varietal (lavandula angustifolia) for a fragrant smell and taste, with the characteristic relaxation and sleep benefits.**

HIBISCUS COOLER

Cold and flu-fighting sweet elderberry and antioxidant-rich tart hibiscus in a honey lemon base is always a winner for a party.

Honey Simple Syrup:

1 c honey

1 c water

Hibiscus Cooler:

1/4 c dried elderberries

6 dried hibiscus flowers

1 c lemon juice

6 c water

Prepare the honey simple syrup by boiling the water and stirring in honey until dissolved. Add the lemon juice, water, elderberries and hibiscus. Let the herbs steep at least two hours. It will turn a beautiful rich pink color (antioxidants at work!). Strain out herbs. Serve chilled.

DR. K'S ANTI-INFLAMMATORY ELIXIR

High in antioxidants, anti-inflammatory compounds and warming to the core, this juice is my go-to for sore muscles or to ward off a cold. For an added anti-inflammatory boost, consider adding 10 mg of a cannabinoid (CBD) oil.

2 tart apples (Granny Smith, Braeburn, Pink Lady, Winesap, Honeycrisp)
2 carrots
1 beet with beet greens
½ inch turmeric root
¼ inch ginger root
Optional: 10 mg CBD oil

Juice in a juicer as per appliance instructions. Alternatively, chop coarsely and place in a blender with 1 C water. Blend and strain the pulp using a cheesecloth or nut milk bag.

SPOTLIGHT: WHAT IS CBD?

Surging in popularity, cannabidiol (CBD) is a cannabis compound that is non-psychoactive. Its terpene-rich anti-inflammatory oil is derived from hemp and does not contain tetrahydrocannabinol (THC) or produce any "high." It is used for a variety of purposes, including insomnia, anxiety, pain and seizures. Given its relative newcomer status, studies are lacking, and much evidence is anecdotal. It's only pharmaceutical use currently is as an anti-seizure drug, which is a much higher dose than is generally used in over the counter preparations. Manufacturing and labeling are largely unregulated. Labels generally will denote how much CBD is in the entire product, leaving the consumer to calculate the number of milligrams per serving. I anticipate the production and labeling will be more regulated in the future as the research expands and hope to see it well researched as an option for the complementary treatment of pain, inflammatory conditions and anxiety.

ADAPTOGENIC ALMOND MILK

Almond milk is delicious, nutritious and easy to make at home. Commercially made nut milks often have fillers and thickeners such as carrageenan (which is associated with colon cancer) and added gums. Making it at home avoids these chemicals and allows for a variety of customization of flavors and herbs. I love the addition of ashwagandha for an extra boost of adaptogenic calm.

1 c raw almonds, soaked in water for 8 hours
2 c water
2 T honey
1 tsp vanilla extract
1 tsp. cinnamon
½ tsp. cardamom
Pinch of nutmeg
Optional: 1 T ashwagandha powder

Combine all ingredients in a blender. Blend until smooth. Strain using a cheesecloth or nut milk bag.

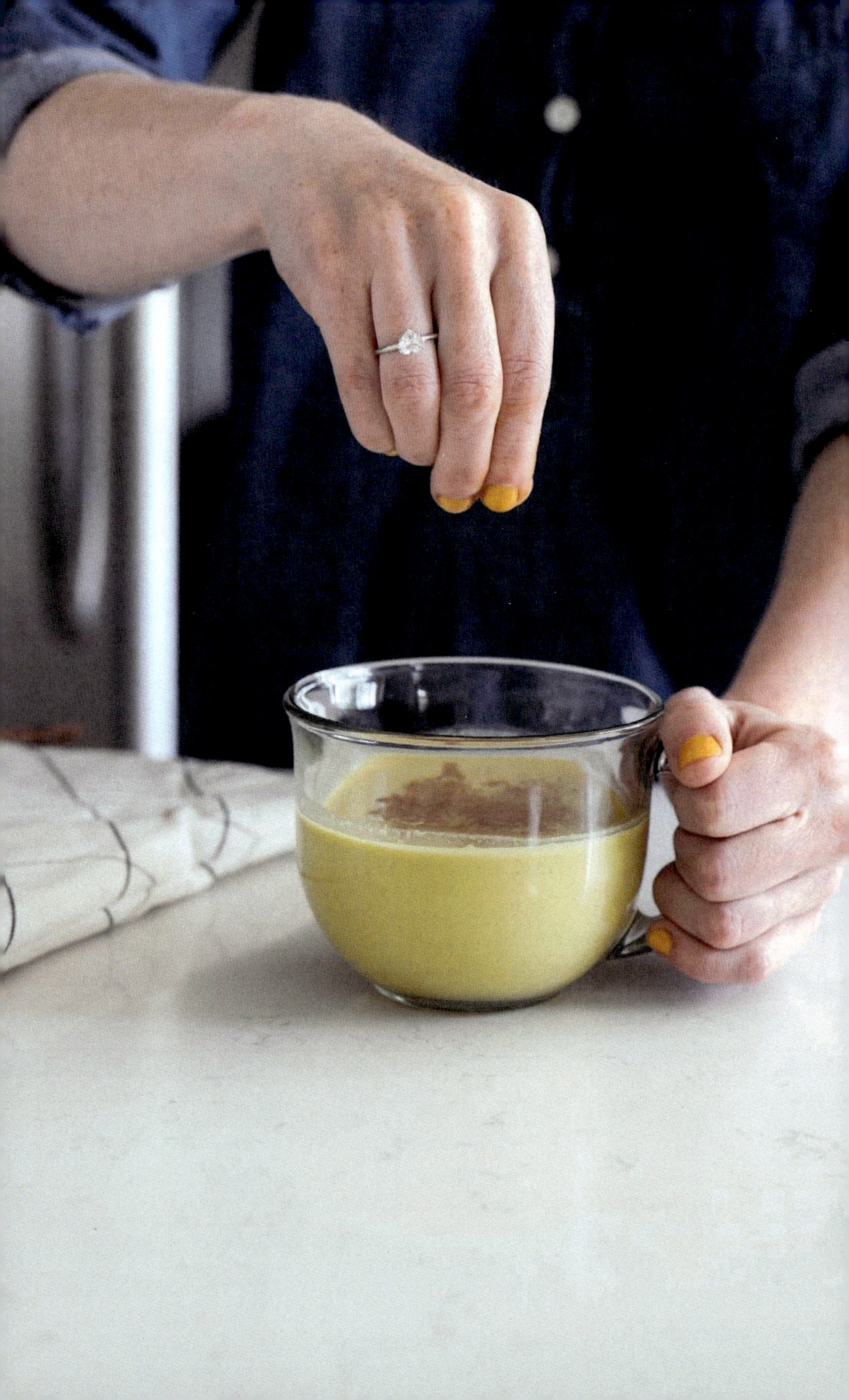

GOLDEN MILK

The adaptogenic almond milk gets an anti-inflammatory upgrade with this golden milk recipe. Golden milk is a traditional Indian beverage, served warm in the evening. It is a nice addition to an evening "wind down" ritual, gives a boost of pain-fighting anti-inflammatory compounds and is warming to the constitution. The pepper contains piperine, a compound shown to increase the systemic absorption of one of turmeric's active anti-inflammatory ingredients, curcumin. Curcumin is known to be antimicrobial, anti-inflammatory, and even protective against cancers. Ancient wisdom for modern healing!

2 c adaptogenic almond milk (previous recipe), oat milk, or coconut milk
¼ inch grated ginger root or ½ T dried ginger powder
½ inch grated turmeric root or 2 T dried turmeric powder
½ tsp cinnamon
½ tsp cardamom

1 tsp vanilla extract

2 T honey

1 pinch of pepper or 4 whole peppercorns

Add all ingredients to a saucepan and stir. Bring to a boil and then simmer for 10 minutes. Strain out herbs and enjoy.

SPICED OAT MILK

Oat milk is a creamy, inexpensive milk alternative that is wonderful enjoyed by itself or as a replacement for dairy in coffee drinks. For those who are sensitive to dairy, oat milk is delicious and easy to make at home. I enjoy the Ayurvedic addition of warming spices along with a touch of natural sweetness.

1 c oats, covered in water and softened for 6-8 hours
2 c filtered water
1 tsp cinnamon
¼ tsp each cardamom, nutmeg, and ginger
1 T honey
1 tsp vanilla extract

Soak the oats and drain excess water. Combine with 2 cups filtered water and blend. Strain the oats using a nut milk bag or cheesecloth, squeezing out the oat milk. Add the spices and honey, stirring to mix. Keep refrigerated. It will naturally separate; shake before use.

ENERGIZING RHODIOLA HIBISCUS TEA

Rhodiola rosea, an adaptogen with a delicate floral flavor, has been used for centuries in Nordic countries. Viking warriors would take this herb on their journeys to counteract fatigue and increase immunity. Now, it is the antidote to twenty-first century fatigue. Studies show that rhodiola leads to statistically significant improvements in fatigue, general well-being, mood stability, motivation, concentration, anxiety, sleep and physical and mental performance. For my patients with low energy, fatigue and mental fog, I recommend rhodiola in the mornings. It is delicious brewed with the floral, tart hibiscus flower, which has been shown to decrease blood pressure and act as a mild diuretic. The honeybush adds a delicious dose of antioxidants. Caffeine-free, but energizing, rhodiola should be taken no later than the early afternoon. This can be enjoyed hot or iced or made into a summer popsicle treat!

1 c honeybush tea

¼ c dried hibiscus flowers

¼ c dried Rhodiola rosea

Brew with 8 cups boiling water, steeping for at least ten minutes. Alternately, brew 2 T tea per 8 oz if a single cup is desired.

PREGNANCY AND POSTPARTUM TEA

This is a tea I routinely gift to an expectant mother during the third trimester. When started at 36 weeks gestation, the red raspberry leaf has been shown to significantly shorten the pushing phase of labor. The shatavari herb (asparagus racemosus) is an Ayurvedic herb traditionally used as a rejuvenative tonic to the female reproductive tract and may help increase breast milk production. Cardamom, a gently warming spice, is grounding and restorative during this unique time.

1 c Shatavari
1 c Red Raspberry Leaf
2 T Cardamom

Combine dry herbs. Brew 2 T loose-leaf herbs per 12 oz. hot water. Drink 24 oz. daily from 36 weeks gestation through the first 6 weeks postpartum.

MOON TEA

This tea blend is used for the regulation of the menstrual cycle and decreasing uncomfortable menstrual symptoms. Cramp bark, aptly named, helps decrease menstrual cramping, while the fennel seeds aid in decreased bloating. Yarrow can be added if heavy menstrual bleeding is a concern.

1 c Red raspberry leaf
1 c Spearmint
¼ c Cramp bark
2 T Fennel
Optional: ¼ c Yarrow

Combine dry herbs. Brew 2 T loose-leaf herbs per 8 oz. hot water. Drink 24 oz. daily during the last two weeks of the menstrual cycle.

MEDICINAL GARDENING SPOTLIGHT: SPEARMINT

Spearmint, a member of the mint family, is delicious in hot and iced teas, and also a great addition to a fruit salad. It is easy to grow outside or in a windowsill. It should be grown in its own container as it can be an invasive species and spread easily.

HERBAL MEDICINE

The notion that gentle medicine is not effective is incorrect. My experience is that herbs can take longer to work, but also have minimal side effects and fewer drug interactions compared to Western medicine. For many concerns when the heavy hand of Western drugs isn't warranted, plants can fulfill the need. We will explore together some remedies to make at home.

Helpful Tools:

Cheesecloth or nut milk bag

Pint and quart mason jars

Coffee grinder

Cheese grater

Double boiler (or can use a stainless bowl or Pyrex dish in a pot of boiling water)

Amber glass jars for storage

Masking tape and pen for labeling

THE BASICS: TINCTURES AND GLYCERITES

Tinctures and glycerites are concentrated herbal extracts. Alcohol is the menstruum or solvent used to prepare tinctures and vegetable glycerin is the solvent used to prepare glycerites. The solvent serves to draw the extract out of the herb. Tinctures and glycerites are concentrated, shelf-stable herbal formulations that are taken orally.

Tinctures will work more effectively to draw out extracts from herbs but can be less palatable for children. Glycerites work well for people avoiding alcohol and children will readily accept the naturally sweet flavor of this type of herbal medicine.

For most dried herbs, 80 to 100 proof alcohol will work well when making a tincture and is readily available as vodka and brandy. Vegetable glycerin is readily available in natural food markets and is diluted to 70% glycerin/30% water for medicine making as a glycerite. I suggest making a batch of glycerite ahead of time so that the mixture will be ready and waiting when you need it. These liquids used to make the tincture or glycerite are called the menstruum. Boil jars prior to use. For a Simpler's Method, cover the dried herbs, filling the jar with the menstruum of choice. This method should not be used with fresh herbs because of the water content; fresh herbs require higher proof grain alcohol to prevent mold. In addition, a more calculated method is needed when using herbs with potential toxicity, to be able to calculate a precise dose. The herbs presented here are extremely safe and amenable to the Simpler's Method.

For dried herbs, generally the jar will be about half full of herbs, leaves or flowers, and one quarter full for berries or barks, which expand more over time. Cover the herbs, filling the jar with the menstruum of choice. Let it sit in a dark cupboard or pantry for two weeks, giving the jar a shake each day and making sure the herbs are fully covered. After two weeks, strain the herbs through a cheesecloth or nut milk bag, kneading them to extract as much liquid as possible. That liquid is your medicine! Store in a dark bottle at room temperature 2+ years for a tincture, and 1 year for a glycerite.

DR. K'S ELDERBERRY ELIXIR

This is one of my very favorite seasonal recipes. Every fall I make this to sip on over the winter, to ward off cold and flu. Elderberries contain a neuraminidase inhibitor to inhibit the influenza virus' replication; its efficacy rivals Tamiflu, the flu treatment medication. The astragalus adds an additional immune boost, along with warming spices and a hint of citrus. It's great on its own or drizzled over a good vanilla ice cream.

½ c dried elderberries
2 T dried astragalus
2-3 pitted, dried plums
1 T orange zest
1 cinnamon stick
1 T cardamom seeds
Brandy (80 to 100 proof)
Pint mason jar

Grind herbs into a coarse powder and place in the mason jar. Add the plums, zest, cinnamon and cardamom. Cover to the top of the jar with brandy. Shake until all herbs are covered and place in a sunny window. Shake every day. Add more liquid as needed to keep the herbs covered. After two weeks, strain out herbs using a cheesecloth or nut milk bag. Return the liquid to a dark glass jar. It will keep for 2+ years at room temperature.

Take 2 teaspoons 2-3 times daily, as needed

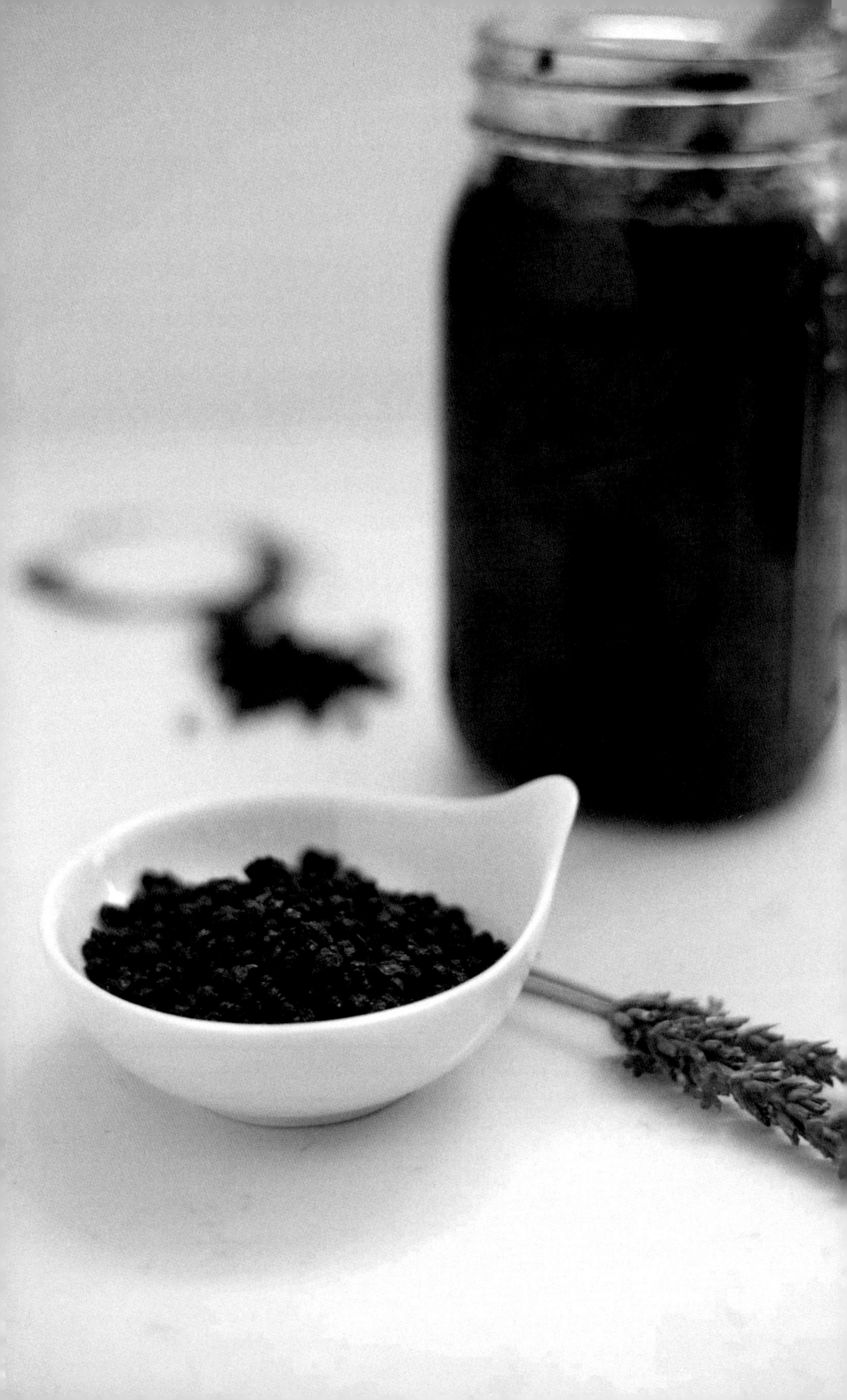

ELDERBERRY POPSICLES

These popsicles are wonderful, especially for kids with a cold and sore throat. They give a gentle boost to the immune system from the elderberry and a natural cough suppressant from the honey, all in a frozen treat that is tasty to eat and eases a sore throat. The syrup is delicious on its own as well. Please note, no honey should be given to a child less than one year of age. The syrup can also be enjoyed on its own, when stored in the fridge.

Elderberry Syrup:
1 c dried elderberries
2 c apple juice
1 c raw honey
Squeeze of lemon juice
1 c water
8 Popsicle molds

Bring elderberries and water to a boil. Gently bruise the berries, encouraging more dark purple color into the syrup. Reduce heat and boil down until it has a thick syrup like consistency. Strain out elderberries. Return to heat source and add honey. Heat and stir until combined. Add lemon juice and water. Stir to combine and place in popsicle molds. Freeze.

DR. K'S HERBAL COUGH SYRUP

Thyme is a natural cough suppressant, on par with over the counter products like Robitussin. Add some oregano for a natural antiseptic. Any honey will work for cough suppression. For an additional antiseptic boost, I prefer manuka honey.

¼ c dried thyme leaves or 4-5 stems of fresh thyme leaves
2 T dried oregano, 3 drops oregano essential oil or 1-2 stems fresh oregano
½ c honey
2 T lemon juice

Pour 1 cup boiling water over the leaves/stems and let it brew as a strong tea for 10 minutes. Strain out herbs. Add honey and lemon. (An adult may enjoy the addition of a shot of whiskey in the syrup.)

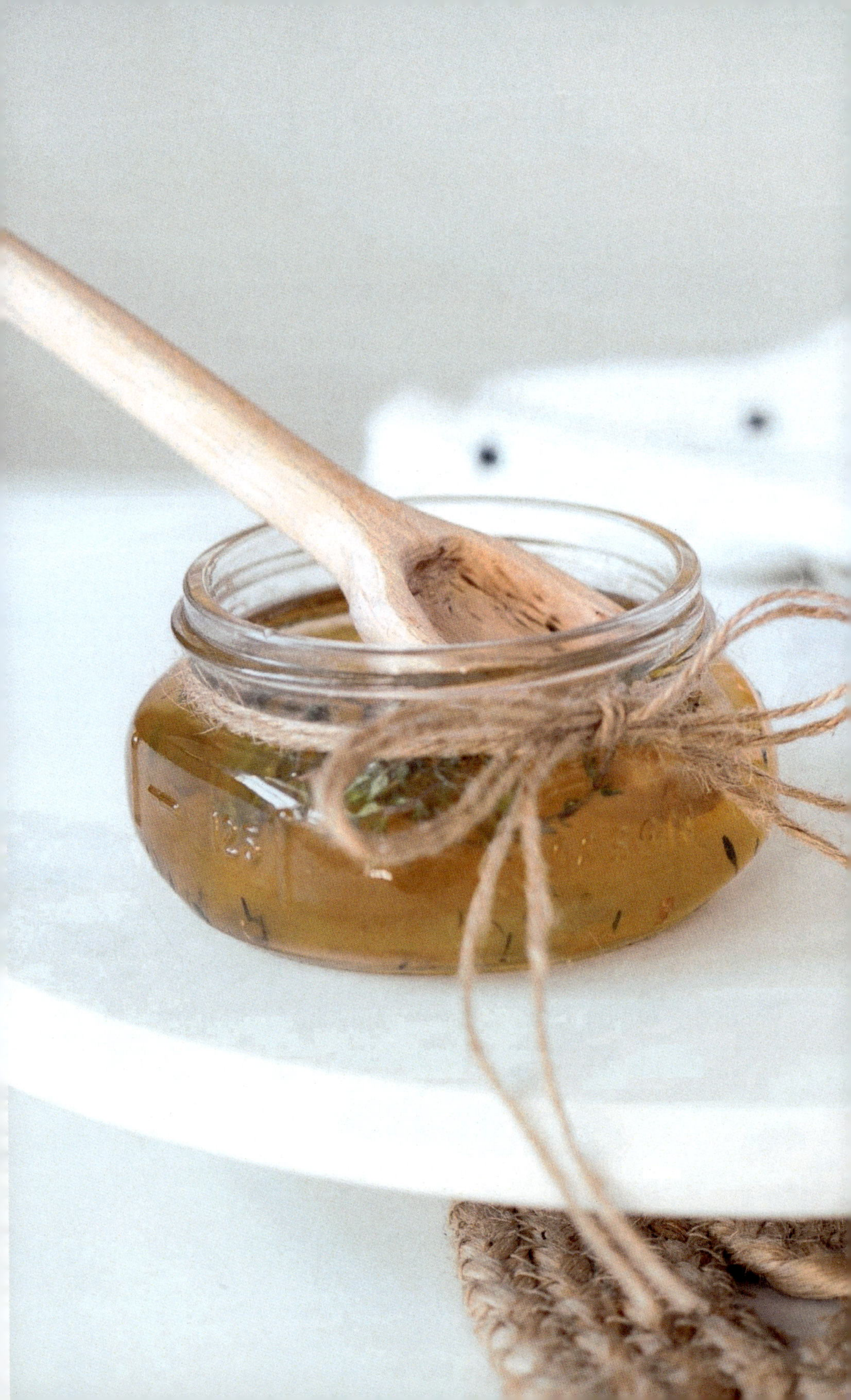

Keep in the refrigerator. Take 1 T by mouth as needed. This is very safe and cannot be overdosed on its alcohol-free form. Do not give honey to infants under 1 year of age.

MEDICINAL GARDENING SPOTLIGHT: THYME

Thyme, a culinary herb with medicinal properties, contains thymol, a powerful antiseptic and is approved for the treatment of cough and upper respiratory infection in the German pharmacopeia. It is a Mediterranean herb and grows well in such a climate, with fairly dry soil and full sun. It will be amenable to growing in a container, even in a windowsill. This is a must-have herb in your garden. There are many varietals; I prefer English thyme for medicine-making and lemon thyme for culinary ventures.

SORE THROAT SALT GARGLE

When I was a little girl, I remember my grandmother making me a warm salt gargle for sore throat. It was instant relief. I've added some herbs to her original recipe. The sage is a natural pain reliever for the throat and the oregano adds a natural antiseptic for viral and bacterial infections. It should be tepid, not hot, and feels wonderfully soothing on a sore throat. This is safe for children to use.

2 stems of oregano (or 2 T dried leaf)
4-6 sage leaves (or ¼ C dried)
¼ c table salt

Pour 2 cups of boiling water over the herbs and let steep for 10 minutes. Strain out the herbs. Mix in the salt until dissolved. Let it cool to tepid. Gargle as desired.

MEDICINAL GARDENING SPOTLIGHT: OREGANO

Oregano, traditionally an Italian herb, grows well in a Mediterranean climate, with relatively dry soil and full sun to partial shade. It will grow nicely in a pot and can be combined with thyme and marjoram in a container. It is a culinary and medicinal herb, with powerful antiseptic properties.

CITRUS SPICED BITTERS AND DIGESTION

We have an epidemic of patients using medications to reduce acid secretion and heartburn, with potential long-term side effects. Many of these digestive issues can be addressed with dietary changes and gentler herbal remedies.

Digestive bitters start working once they hit the bitter receptors on the tongue. They stimulate the stomach, gallbladder and pancreas to secrete acid, bile and enzymes to break down food properly and assist in the absorption of nutrients. They can ease occasional heartburn and indigestion and decrease gas and bloating with a meal. These have been used for centuries; even old-fashioned horehound candy was originally designed for digestion!

¼ c Dandelion leaf
¼ c Horehound
½ inch grated Ginger root
1 T citrus zest
1 tsp. Cinnamon
1 tsp. Cardamom
1 c Spiced Rum

Place all ingredients in a mason jar and cover with rum to the top. Shake every day for two weeks, making sure herbs remain covered. Strain out the herbs. Take 1 T of the liquid prior to a meal; or it can be mixed in warm water to make an aperitif.

IMMUNITY OXYMEL ELIXIR

An oxymel is a delicious way to take herbs. "Oxymel," from the Latin word *oxymeli* (meaning "acid and honey") is a centuries-old medicinal used to make herbs palatable. Oxymel can be taken by the spoonful or in warm water for a cold, or it doubles as a tasty salad dressing and marinade for chicken. This is a winter staple in my house for boosting immunity and cold prevention and treatment.

1 mason jar
Fill ¼ of the jar with equal parts dried rosemary, oregano and thyme
1 T lemon zest
2 cloves peeled garlic
Fill the rest of the jar with 1:1 ratio of honey and apple cider vinegar
Let steep in a dark place for two weeks, shaking the jar daily. Strain out herbs and garlic. It will keep shelf stable all season.

INFUSED HONEYS

To make herbal honeys, fresh herbs or dried and powdered herbs can be used. If fresh, stir coarsely chopped herb into the honey. Let sit for two weeks. Warm the honey in a glass jar gently by placing in a pan of hot water to thin it and make it easier to strain. Strain the herbs out. If dried and powdered, the herb can be stirred into the honey and does not need to be strained out. Keep honey at room temperature.

LAVENDER HONEY

1 c raw, local honey

¼ c lavender flowers

This is my go-to for an amazing cheese plate. Drizzled over manchego or gouda with some nuts and dried fruit, this is the ultimate addition to a cheese plate and wine. It is also calming and can be stirred into a cup of hot chamomile or lemon balm tea for additional anti-anxiety help to wind down at night.

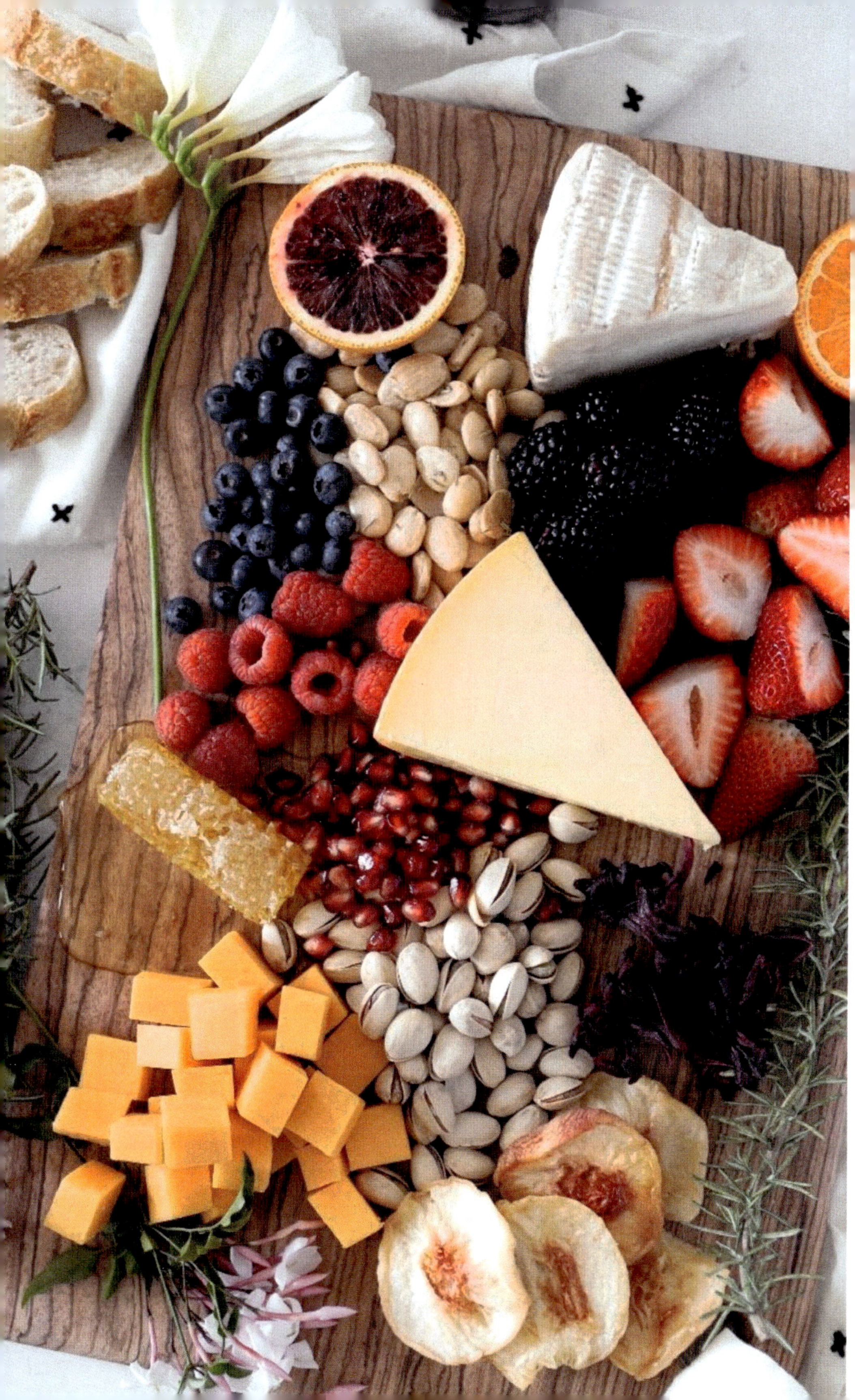

ADAPTOGEN HONEY

1 c raw honey
2 T powdered ashwagandha
1 tsp. vanilla extract
1 tsp. pumpkin pie spices (cinnamon, cardamom, nutmeg, cloves, ginger)

Warming spices, smooth vanilla and adaptogenic herbal medicine wrapped up in a sweet package; this honey is just divine. Stir all ingredients until combined. Spread on toast, drizzle on oatmeal or almond butter and sliced apples, or dissolve in Best Rest tea for a good night's sleep. It's a delicious way to add some calming adaptogen to life.

SPOTLIGHT: ASHWAGANDHA

This jewel of Ayurvedic herbs is one of my very favorite for women's medicine. This herb can be used in a variety of forms, in teas, tinctures, powders in cooking, or taken in capsules. It should be used at night, gently encouraging the body to relax and let go of stress. Termed an adaptogen because of its ability to help the body manage stress, ashwagandha modulates the release of cortisol, the body's stress hormone, allowing the body to rest. Ashwagandha also has a mild effect on improving thyroid function, often optimizing function for patients with mild or subclinical hypothyroidism.

SAGE AND THYME HONEY

This is a must for cold season. The sage is an excellent pain reliever for a sore throat and thyme and honey both act as cough suppressants. Have this on-hand all year. It works as well as over the counter cough suppressants but is completely natural. Sage sun tea is also excellent for the relief of hot flashes and excessive sweating.

1 c raw, local honey

¼ c chopped sage and thyme leaves, fresh or dried

Take 1 T by mouth as needed

MEDICINAL GARDENING SPOTLIGHT: SAGE

Salvia officinalis, or common sage, is a perennial, evergreen shrub that is a member of the mint family. It is low maintenance and drought tolerant. It will grow well in a sunny, well-drained spot in the ground or can share a pot with other Mediterranean herbs such as rosemary and thyme. Sage has both culinary and medicinal use as a cooking herb and for pain relief and wound healing.

SKIN HONEY

This is excellent for eczema, skin irritations and wound healing. Manuka honey and sage actually prevent infection and speed healing when placed over a wound. It is soothing and will provide relief of irritation and pain.

1 c Manuka honey
¼ c chopped sage leaves
¼ c chopped comfrey leaves
10 drops cedarwood essential oil
10 drops lavender essential oil

Combine all ingredients and allow herbs to infuse for two weeks. Strain out herbs. Apply liberally to affected area.

MEDICINAL GARDENING SPOTLIGHT: COMFREY

Comfrey is not a common garden plant, but it is easily grown and endlessly helpful for managing the cuts and scrapes of life. The leaves and roots contain allantoin, which speeds healing and tissue growth. Comfrey attracts pollinators and is nature's answer to organic fertilizer; a perfect addition to a garden. The leaves can be used in salves and honeys, along with the root. When the plant has been harvested, it can be used for mulch due to its high nutrient content. It can be planted in the ground or a pot and enjoys well-drained soil with full sun to partial shade.

PEPPERMINT SKIN COMPRESS

This is a very simple recipe that is wonderful for itchy skin. It works wonders on itchy bug bites, poison oak, eczema itching and any skin irritation. This can also be placed on the temples, neck, and forehead to soothe a headache. In studies, peppermint oil worked as well as ibuprofen for mild to moderate headache. Please be sure to keep the oil away from eyes.

1 c ice water
5 drops peppermint oil

Dip a cotton cloth in the mixture and apply to affected area.

NATURAL BODY SCRUB

This is so indulgent, hydrating and polishing for the skin. Sugar will be gentler on the "scrubbing", while salt is more rough. The basic recipe is one-part oil to two parts sugar or salt, with some fun optional add-ins, depending on preference. I prefer olive or coconut oil for this recipe, with olive oil being particularly good for sensitive or eczematous skin. This scrub is also great for dry lips.

1 c oil (coconut, jojoba, sunflower, and kukui nut oils all work well)
2 c sea salt or cane sugar

Optional add-ins:
2 T lemon juice for extra antioxidants and exfoliation
Crushed mint leaves for awakening
Pumpkin pie spices and brown sugar instead of cane sugar for an autumn scrub
Green tea leaves for decreasing redness

NATURAL DEODORANT

I have experimented with many natural deodorant recipes, and this is my favorite. The coconut oil and tea tree oil are naturally antimicrobial, reducing odor, and the arrowroot dries without being irritating like a higher proportion of baking soda. The shea butter will warm in your fingers and make it easy to apply.

3 T unrefined coconut oil
2 T shea butter
1/4 c arrowroot starch
2 T baking soda
5 drops tea tree oil

Combine all ingredients and keep in a small glass jar. Apply with fingertips.

THE BASICS: INFUSED OILS

Infused oils are a wonderful addition to a hot bath, in homemade body products, or in culinary use and are very simple to make. Fill a mason jar ¾ full with dried herbs and cover with an oil. For topical use, I like sunflower oil as it is naturally high in Vitamin E, not greasy, and absorbs well into the skin. Jojoba, sesame, and coconut oils are also good choices and can be mixed to make your own signature blend.

Place the covered jar in the sun for two to four weeks, shaking daily to keep the herbs covered. Strain the herbs out using a cheesecloth or nut milk bag. The infused oil is shelf stable and can be used on its own or in salves.

If you need an infused oil faster, a crock-pot can be of use. Place the herbs and oil in the crock-pot and cook on low for 8 hours. Strain the herbs as above.

THE BASICS: MAKING A SALVE

Salves are wonderfully easy to make, and many varieties can be used as natural medicine, from a breath-easy salve for a child's cough to a calming one for eczema. Infuse oils with the herbs needed for the particular purpose you are trying to address. Take the infused oil and heat it gently in a double boiler. Add grated beeswax. Add a hydrating shea or cocoa butter if desired, which makes the salve a little easier to apply. Add any essential oils desired. Take a spoonful out and stick in the freezer for a few minutes and test the consistency. If it's too hard, add a little more oil. If it's too mushy, add another tablespoon or two of beeswax. Pour into tins and let it set at room temperature.

We will discuss some different herbs for salve making, but once you know the basics, you can create your own!

HAPPY SKIN SALVE

As an obstetrician, I created this recipe for the countless women I have treated with sore bottoms after birth and who need something to soothe cracked and chapped nipples. This is also an excellent salve for hemorrhoids during pregnancy, for eczema, and for diaper rash. Calendula is wonderfully soothing and healing, along with chamomile. The lavender is soothing and anti-inflammatory, and the sunflower oil absorbs well and is moisturizing, while shea butter adds a layer of skin protection.

2 c sunflower oil infused with ½ c each dried calendula and chamomile
10 drops lavender essential oil
½ c grated beeswax
½ c shea butter
1 tsp Vitamin E oil

Infuse the oil with the herbs for two weeks, shaking periodically. Strain out herbs using a nut milk bag or cheesecloth. Using a double boiler, gently heat the oil and stir in the beeswax and shea butter until melted. Add the essential oil. Pour into small mason jars and let cool.

ECZEMA SALVE

All the ingredients in this eczema salve are skin soothing and healing! Calendula soothes and reduces redness. In studies, chamomile applied topically alleviated eczema as well as low dose hydrocortisone, without any of the undesired steroid adverse effects. Cedarwood oil acts as an anti-inflammatory and reduces the unpleasant dryness that tends to accompany eczema. While this has limited data, I often will open a probiotic capsule and add the contents to the oil. Anecdotally I have seen this improve symptoms of eczema and is a safe option to try.

½ c each jojoba and sunflower oils infused with ½ c calendula
1/3 c grated beeswax
¼ c shea butter
2 T coconut oil
10 drops cedarwood essential oil
1 tsp Vitamin E oil

Infuse the oil with the herbs for two weeks, shaking periodically. Strain out herbs using a nut milk bag or cheesecloth. Using a double boiler, gently heat the oil and stir in the beeswax and shea butter until melted. Add the essential oil. Pour into small mason jars and let cool.

COUGH SALVE

The minty menthol of this salve acts as a natural chest rub for cough, congestion and cold. A little applied under the nostrils will help to naturally open up the sinus passages.

1 c sunflower oil
1/3 c grated beeswax
¼ c shea butter
10 drops peppermint essential oil
10 drops eucalyptus essential oil
1 tsp Vitamin E oil

Infuse the oil with the herbs for two weeks, shaking periodically. Strain out herbs using a nut milk bag or cheesecloth. Using a double boiler, gently heat the oil and stir in the beeswax and shea butter until melted. Add the essential oil. Pour into small mason jars and let cool.

POSTPARTUM SOAK

I created this soak after a lactation consultant suggested a saltwater soak for sore nipples postpartum. Since then, I've recommended it to countless patients, who report immediate relief. It soothes the painful, raw skin that mamas get on their bottoms after giving birth, as well as on the nipples when breastfeeding in those early days. Calendula is an herbal skin-soother, and arnica flowers decrease pain. The salts decrease swelling, pain and infection risk. This is safe to use as often as needed. Gently pat to dry after soaking and leave the affected area open to air as much as possible.

½ c calendula flower
½ c arnica flower
2 c sea salt
2 c Epsom salt
Grind herbs. Add to salts. Mix all ingredients and store.

For breast soak, dissolve ¼ C salt mixture in 2 C warm water. Divide into two bowls and submerge nipples in the solution.

For herbal sitz bath, add 2 cups salt mixture to 2 inches of warm water in a tub.

TOXINS IN THE HOME

Our home is where we sleep, eat and raise our families. It's also where a majority of toxic exposures can occur – in our cleaning and personal care products, furniture, carpets and paints. Here are some suggestions to minimize toxic home exposures and a few of my personal nontoxic clean recipes. A good resource for more information is the Environmental Working Group at www.ewg.org. They provide a registry with information about specific personal care and home cleaning products to help you make informed choices.

Furniture

You are spending at least 1/3 of your life on your mattress and couch. Make sure the foam is Certi-Pur certified and avoid polyurethane foam when possible. "Memory foam" tends to emit gas more and should be avoided unless Certi-Pur certified and from non petroleum sources. Latex is a safe choice, although more expensive. Pocketed coil technology has improved the feel of innerspring mattresses and is a safe choice. Choose non-chemical fire retardants such as wool, silica and rayon in a mattress. Greenguard and Greenguard Gold certifications are a top choice in mattress ratings. This is especially important for children's mattresses, as children exhibit higher levels of flame retardants in their blood than do adults when tested.

Look for GOTS (Global Organic Textile Standard) and Oeko-Tex® certifications to make the safest choices for textiles used in furniture. Products with these certifications have become more available in recent years, with Ikea and Target offering several choices. Avoid any stain pretreatment or "Scotch Guard" on fabrics.

Choose solid wood over wood laminate and particle board/pressed board when possible. The composite woods are typically pressed together with formaldehyde, a known human carcinogen. Pay particular attention to cribs and other children's furniture items, as children's bedrooms often exceed safe formaldehyde levels.

Flooring

Carpeting should be low VOC (Volatile Organic Compound), preferably Greenguard certified. Padding should be wool or felt, when possible and secured with a low VOC adhesive to avoid PFC (perfluorinated chemicals), PVC (polyvinyl chloride) and phthalates exposure. Avoid any stain or waterproofing treatment products as these contain perfluorinated chemicals, which are classified as a likely carcinogen. Tile and natural wood flooring are preferable. Look for a low VOC sealant on wood flooring. As with furniture, avoid composite woods that emit formaldehyde. These recommendations are especially important for families with young children, as babies spend more time in direct contact with the floor and have been shown to exhibit these chemicals in relatively high concentration by the age of two.

Paint

Look for Green Seal-11 certified paint, water based latex paints and low or no VOC paints. Avoid any formaldehyde releasing paints. When painting, work in a well-ventilated area. Consider "milk paint" (nontoxic water-based paint) for painting children's furniture.

Kitchen Items

Use glass or stainless-steel water bottles to avoid petroleum chemicals that can leach into the water of single-use water bottles and to avoid contributing to plastics pollution on the earth. I prefer these over even BPA-free reusable bottles, as these may still have harmful plastic chemicals.

Never heat in plastic. Use glass. Replace a plastic microwave steamer with a glass Pyrex bowl or a silicone "steamer" lid. Use stainless steel reusable containers for kids' lunch items. They are dishwasher safe and virtually indestructible. Reusable produce bags are inexpensive, help keep produce fresher and cut down the impact of single-use plastic on our environment.

Avoid all nonstick pans, regardless of safety claims. Once scratched, these release fluorinated chemicals into your food. A well-seasoned cast iron pan is naturally nonstick and inexpensive. Cook food in stainless steel, cast iron or enameled cast iron. Bake in silicone or stainless-steel trays covered with parchment paper for ease of cleaning.

Food

Food can linings often contain BPA (bisphenol A) or BPS (bisphenol S). Avoid canned foods when possible, especially when they contain acidic food like tomatoes. Choose jarred or boxed versions or a trusted canning companies like Eden Foods and Westbrae Naturals that does not use plasticized liners.

Use a carbon water filter. They are inexpensive and can be the kind in a separate pitcher or installed in a refrigerator water and ice system.

PERSONAL CARE PRODUCTS

Sunscreen

For the sake of our coral reefs and human health, avoid chemical sunscreens made with oxybenzone, avobenzone, octisalate, octocrylene, homosalate, octinoxate and the worst, (and most pervasive), oxybenzone. Oxybenzone has a direct hormonal effect and is absorbed readily through the skin. Once discontinued, blood levels of the chemical drop dramatically. Choose mineral sunscreen consisting of zinc and titanium and use sunscreen as a last resort. Favor UPF clothes to cover skin, avoiding sun during peak times of 10 am to 2 pm, find shade and wear sunglasses.

Deodorant

Choose non-aluminum products and avoid "antiperspirants." Perspiring is a healthy way to regulate temperature and shed toxins. Better to keep an extra shirt on hand than to avoid sweating. I prefer Lume deodorant, Schmidts, Native or the homemade deodorant listed in this book.

Cosmetics and Body Products

Choose mineral products, when possible. Not only do these have fewer toxins, they provide some mineral-based sunscreen as well. Avoid "long lasting" lipsticks and chemical sunscreens in cosmetic products. Avoid any added "fragrance" as these often contain phthalates. Use non-chemical moisturizers such as coconut oil and shea butter. Check the database at www.ewg.org/skindeep for specific product recommendations. Avoid sulfates in shampoos when possible. Avoid parabens in facial soaps and lotions. In hand soap, avoid anything that is advertised as "antibacterial" and avoid triclosan as an ingredient, which is associated with hormonal disruption.

Home Products

Avoid any added fragrances to cleaning supplies or laundry detergents since they are typically derived from chemicals rather than natural ingredients. Avoid dryer sheets as these are particularly loaded with harmful chemicals. Use natural wool balls in the dryer instead. If you prefer a scent to your clothing, sprinkle a few drops of an essential oil of your choice onto the wool balls prior to drying.

Avoid wall "plug-ins", spray air fresheners, and heated wax fragrances for home fragrance, along with car air fresheners. A reed or ultrasonic diffuser with natural essential oils eliminates the chemical concerns, although may still contribute to indoor pollution for a sensitive person with asthma or allergies.

Mop with a steam mop, sprinkling a few drops of lemon and tea tree essential oils on the mop surface. This will effectively disinfect and clean floors without harmful chemicals.

Avoid fragranced garbage bags. Vacuum carpets with a HEPA filter to reduce dust pollution as much as possible. Most surfaces (countertops, bathroom and kitchen) can be cleaned with very simple, nontoxic home recipes included here. For purchased products, look for recommendations in the EWG Guide to Healthy Cleaning developed by the Environmental Working Group (www.ewg.org), as there are many good nontoxic options available.

HEALTHY HOME CLEANER

I use this spray on my kitchen countertops, bathroom sinks, toilets and tile floors. It's a workhorse that cleans well with no toxic ingredients.

16 oz spray bottle
8 oz white vinegar
6 oz water
1 oz rubbing alcohol
1 T castile soap
10 drops lemon essential oil
10 drops tea tree oil

Combine all ingredients in the spray bottle. Use liberally as desired.

NATURAL SOFT SCRUB

If I need a soft scrub cleaner for a stubborn stain in the kitchen, I make up a batch of this. If there is some left over, it will keep in the fridge and can be rehydrated by adding a few more tablespoons of water, if needed.

1 T castile soap
½ c baking soda
3-4 T of water
10 drops lemon essential oil

MIND/BODY MEDICINE

Breathing is the fastest way to hack the nervous system. For most of us, we experience the "fight, flight, freeze" response of our sympathetic nervous system many times each day as we check our phones, navigate traffic, and generally respond to stimuli coming from multiple sources at once. No wonder sleep disturbance is so prevalent in our society. Beyond insomnia, I see this constant nervous system activation contributes to functional abdominal pain, irritable bowel syndrome and central sensitization disorders such as fibromyalgia, as well as the newer concept of adrenal burnout. In my practice, I also see chronic stress and nervous system activation contributes to autoimmunity and fatigue-related disorders.

Here are some of the quickest ways I've found to down regulate the "fight-flight-freeze" response and activate your body's natural ability to rest and restore. Try one of these exercises for three minutes a day for a week, perhaps before bed. Over a relatively short period of time, neuroplasticity- the ability of the neurons to fire and wire together- can change the brain. We can literally reprogram our brain to observe, rather than react, to outside stimuli. This change in neural perception leads to a more gentle, less reactive experience to life. Protective against burnout, stress, insomnia, and improving sleep and restful states, the observation of breath can have a profound impact on daily experience.

Meditation Apps

There are a number of good meditation apps on the market. These can be a great way to be introduced to meditation and develop a practice:

Headspace

Insight Timer

Curable- meditation for treatment of chronic pain

Deep Sleep with Andrew Johnson

10% Happier: Meditation for Fidgety Skeptics

DoYogaWithMe.com

THE 4-7-8 BREATH

If I could choose one routine in this book for my patients to do every day, this would be it. There is nothing else as beneficial for the body as this breathing exercise to lower stress hormones, inflammation and develop good mental health. I learned about this exercise from my mentor, Dr. Andrew Weil and I remain convinced it is the single most impactful thing I can teach my patients to do. It has even been shown in studies to be as effective as anti-anxiety medication!

Do at least four rounds, but no more than eight. I find it is particularly effective when combined with "legs up the wall" pose.

Inhale through your nose for four counts.
Hold your breath for seven counts.

Exhale with your mouth open with your tongue pressed behind your top teeth for eight counts, making a "whooshing" sound as you exhale.

THE THREE-PART BREATH

The three-part breath is another one of my favorite breathing exercises to induce calm and focus. This exercise is done traditionally while lying down although any position may be effective. Both the inhale and exhale are divided into three parts.

On the inhale through the nose, consciously breathe into the pelvis, then the belly, then the chest. You will feel the abdomen rise towards the ceiling and the ribs expand in all dimensions. The exhale through the nose reverses the process, with the ribs deflating with the lungs, then the belly dropping back towards the spine and then the pelvic fullness on release. I routinely recommend it to my patients during labor. I think the combination of the focus, body awareness and deep breathing is very effective for relaxation and pain relief.

THE CIRCULAR BREATH

This is a yogic breath that I learned that works particularly well with forward bends to calm the nervous system. The inhale is through the nose for a deep breath with a slight pause at the top and then exhale through the mouth with a slight pause at the bottom. The inhales and exhales are equivalent in length. I like to visualize the ocean with this breath, the inhale being the wave drawing upwards ready to crash, the exhale being the crashing waves rushing toward shore. I will even visualize this with the waves rising up my back and then crashing over my head, relaxing the entire body with the exhale. While this can be done in any position, try it with a gentle forward fold, knees bent arms either supported on a chair or hanging with the weight of the head. It can feel good to gently shift back and forth, side to side.

> "The tides are in our veins."
> –Robinson Jeffers

THE BOX BREATH

This technique was taught to me by my meditation teacher, who learned that it was taught to Navy SEALs and other high stress military professionals. Indeed, in the emergent moments of my own job as a physician and surgeon, I have found it tremendously helpful in the moment to steady my mind and hands, and enable me to respond in the moment, rather than react out of fear. The technique is quite simple.

Imagine that you are drawing a box in your head. Inhale for a count of 4, drawing a line up. Hold the breath for a count of 4, drawing the line across. Exhale for a count of 4 drawing the line down, and hold for a count of 4, completed the square.

Repeat for at least 8 rounds, if possible.

ENERGY BREATH

This is my go-to to wake up, to inject more energy and vitality into my day. You'll feel silly at first, but it is worth trying. It's the perfect prescription for combating the mid-afternoon slump.

It is a combination of three inhales and then a loud exhale, combined with movement.

Arms out to the side (INHALE through the nose)
Arms up (INHALE again)
Arms out to the side (INHALE again)
Arms down as you squat down (EXHALE through the mouth with a 'Ha' sound). Repeat at least four times.

LEGS UP THE WALL POSE

Viparita karani, or legs up the wall pose, is a restorative yoga posture. I recommend that patients with anxiety and insomnia perform this for five minutes before bed. It is also good for patients with leg swelling and venous stasis, to improve circulation and facilitate the return of blood back to the heart. The increased blood volume in the heart actually causes the atrial receptors to stretch, triggering the parasympathetic nervous system to induce a state of calm and relaxation. Biohacking the nervous system to create more ease in life!

DR. KENNARD'S YIN YOGA FOR SLEEP

Keep the lights in the room dim and play soothing music. Make sure all of the tasks for the day are done, so you can slip right into bed when the practice is done. I actually like performing this practice in bed. It is a welcome shift between the waking and dreaming worlds. Hold each pose for about three minutes. You will notice a difference in your ability to fall asleep and in the quality of your sleep after this practice.

For support, use a stack of folded blankets or a yoga bolster, as pictured.

Sequence:

Viparita karani, legs up the wall pose.

Supported baddha konasana; on your back, supported, in butterfly pose. You may benefit from a pillow or stack of blankets supporting the knees so you can fully relax.

Twists. Lay on the bolster or folded blankets. Bring the knees over to the right side at first. Hold for three minutes. Gently, help the legs to the opposite side and hold for an additional 3 minutes.

Child's pose, supporting yourself with the bolster.

MEDITATION

I think of meditation as becoming an observer of thoughts, rather than a thinker of thoughts. When we are able to observe thoughts, we possess the ability to not automatically engage with them. In this space comes room for the awareness of our true selves; who we really are, what we need in life and the ability to truly relax. Meditation is a powerful prescription against anxiety, panic, depression, insomnia and fear.

Mindful meditation is the most common type of meditation in the Western world. Mindfulness meditation has been adapted in medicine to form the foundation of the mindfulness-based stress reduction program. This program is used in pain, trauma, childbirth, parenting and work stress applications, among others. If you or a loved one is expecting a baby, I highly recommend *Mindful Birthing* by Nancy Bardacke, CNM, who adapted mindfulness-based stress reduction for labor support.

Many activities can be mindful; meditation doesn't have to be done on a zafu cushion. Any repetitive activity with focused attention in the present moment will induce a meditative state. Our grandmothers knitted, and rosaries and malas have been used for centuries. While exercise can be meditative, I believe that the benefits of meditation stem from the upregulation of the parasympathetic nervous system which can only be done when at rest, not while actively exercising. These "recipes" are some beginning approaches to meditation that I routinely prescribe to my patients.

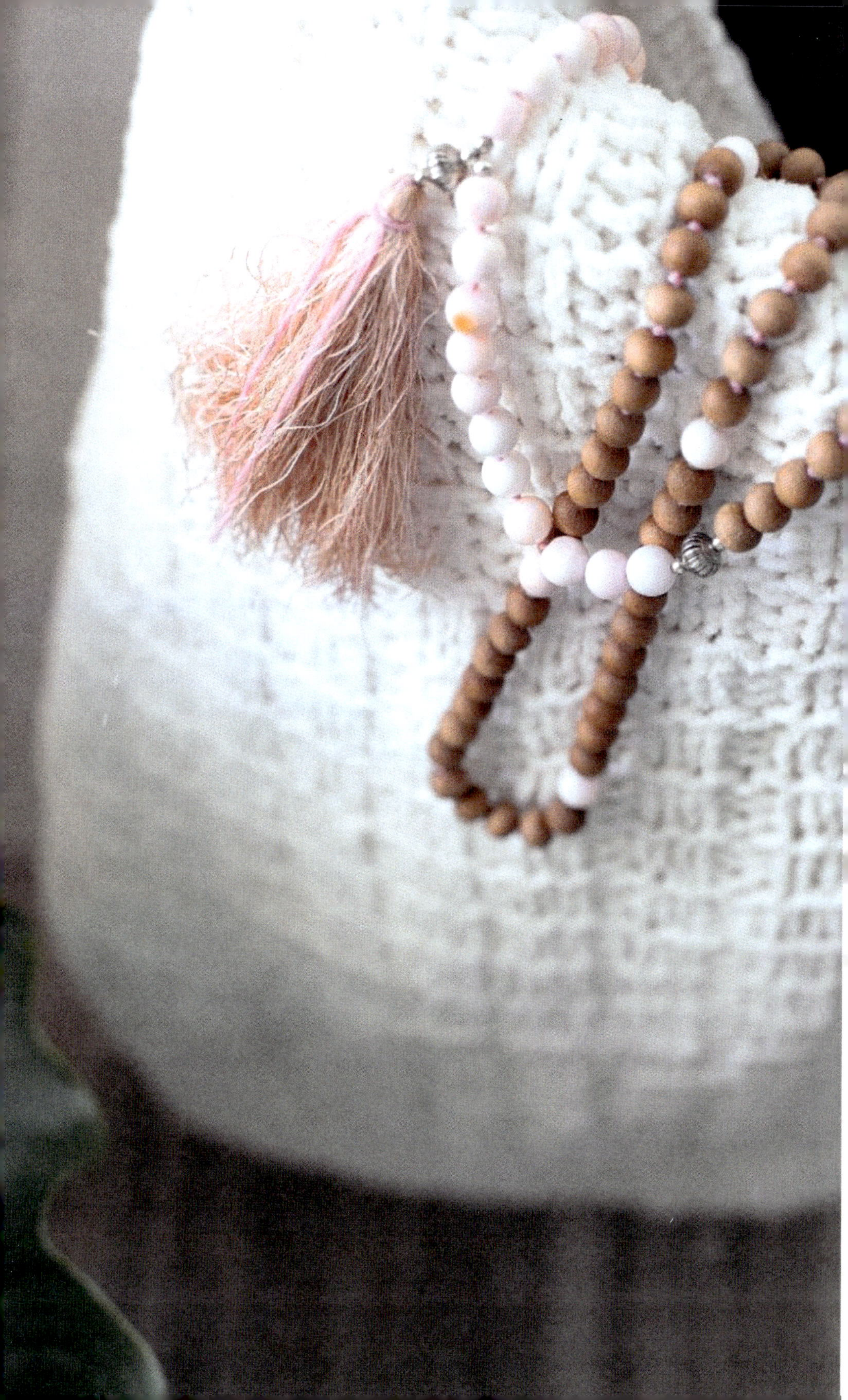

AWARENESS MEDITATION

I think that awareness meditation is the best intro to meditation there is. This is the first step to experiencing the phenomenon of becoming an observer of thoughts, rather than a thinker of thoughts.

Sit comfortably with your hips elevated above knees for comfort. Feel your sitz bones supporting you, pushing into the ground. Imagine the spine is long, like a string of pearls suspended from the ceiling. Notice the breath. Inhale, letting cool air enter the nose. Exhale and the warm air will exit. Notice any bodily sensations or discomforts. Acknowledge these. Thoughts will come up. Allow yourself to observe them and let them go. Sometimes it can be helpful to imagine them floating away down a river.
Set a timer. Try for one minute to start, working up to about ten minutes.

COUNTED BREATH MEDITATION

This meditation is very simple. Without changing your breathing pattern, count 1 as you inhale, 2 as you exhale and so on until you reach 5. Restart at 1 with the cycle of the breath. You will know when your attention wanders when you find yourself at 6…or 20! If you do, just restart at 1. Meditation is the practice of bringing the wandering mind back into the present moment and this exercise is perfect for that.

SIX SENSES MEDITATION

This is one of my favorite short meditations. It can be done anywhere and is quite effective at bringing awareness to the present moment. Grounding in the body and breath, the skill of presence is practiced; giving space to choose a response, rather than react. In this way, we can shape our own experience. This is one of my favorite transitions to do when coming home from work or settling in for bed.

Sit comfortably and let the eyes gently close or unfocus. Focus on your five senses, one at a time.

What can you hear, near and far?
What do you smell?
What are the tastes, inside the mouth?
What do you see; shadows of light or darkness?
What touch do you feel; the touch of clothes, a blanket, or the floor?

Then shift into the sixth sense, the observation of mental activities. Thoughts are natural and the goal is not to get rid of them. Rather, observe them. Allow them to pass along like water in a river going over a waterfall. What else comes along?

This allows us to practice becoming an "observer" of thoughts, rather than a "thinker" of thoughts, providing space to choose a response to those thoughts.

MALA MEDITATION

A mala is a necklace with 108 beads, typically with individual knots between each bead. Sit comfortably just as you did for the awareness meditation. Inhale and exhale with each bead. Some choose to repeat a mantra or a word with each bead. I find that the action of twisting a bead helps keep me grounded and my mind from wandering. It has been used for thousands of years in the Buddhist tradition.

LOVING-KINDNESS MEDITATION

Loving-kindness, or metta, meditation is such a lovely type of meditation. My natural inclination initially was that this type of meditation should be directed towards others. After all, it is our work to offer love and compassion to others. But I find that the first application of this meditation should be toward self. It is bold and necessary to offer yourself compassion and love, and this is an accessible way to do that. I found with my patients that many of the frustrations brought up in women's related issues are compounded by a lack of self-care, self-compassion and self-love. I offer this exercise to patients to encourage them to connect with their own bodies and souls in a positive manner. Once the practitioner feels she is ready to turn this energy outward, it should be turned to a person that is easy to love. Compassion and lovingkindness sent to a best friend, a loved one, family member or a child. Once this neural circuit has been strengthened by weeks of sending love to self and sending love to a loved one, it becomes easier. It will become easier to offer loving kindness towards a person to whom you feel neutral or a person that you do not like. It is a more advanced version of the practice to offer loving kindness to someone that you do not like at all.

This is a good application of the mala meditation practice, where the mantra below is repeated with each bead, eventually replacing "I" with the name of a loved one, and then the name of someone who is difficult for the meditator.

May I be well, happy and peaceful
May I be free from physical and mental suffering
In all areas of my life, may I be well accomplished.
"We don't sit in meditation to become good meditators. We sit in meditation so that we'll be more awake in our lives."
–Pema Chodron

BEE BREATH MEDITATION

Bhramari breath, or "bee" breath, meditation is excellent for relieving grief and anxiety. If the mind is busy and a more focused meditation would be difficult, this is a good option. The noise of the "buzzing" can drown out the endless loops of thoughts in the mind and prepare it for rest. It quickly upregulates the parasympathetic nervous system to decrease anxiety and promote a calmer state of being.

Sit or lie comfortably. Close the eyes. Relax the face and jaw. Take a big breath in and with the lips sealed, exhale and create a forceful "mmmm" buzzing noise. Don't be afraid of volume; use your diaphragm to really move the energy. You'll notice that it almost starts to feel like your skull and body begin to reverberate with the buzzing and the noise is reminiscent of a bee buzzing around your being. Your voice may change tone or crack, but this is natural and a part of processing emotion in the meditation. Try it for eight breaths in a row and then return to your normal breathing. Notice how it has changed. Try another eight breaths. A few minutes of this exercise will leave you in a relaxed, calm state.

FLASHLIGHT MEDITATION

This is a very simple, lovely visualization exercise. Sit comfortably. Push the sitz bones into the surface on which you are seated, creating a long spine. Imagine that someone is holding a flashlight over your head, with the light beaming down on your body in a teepee like fashion. Imagine this warm light washing over your body, on any places with stuck energy or pain, physical or emotional. It could represent the warm love of your loved ones, both here and in the past, or a divine light. Sit in this light and experience the feeling of being safe and calm.

ACKNOWLEDGEMENTS

I thank my dear friend and mentor Dr. Nicole Swiner, for her expertise and help in making this dream a reality through Swiner Publishing Company.

To my photographer Alissa Ellett, at Waypoint Photography, for her beautiful photography that made my cooking come alive.

To my mentors, Drs. Tieraona Low Dog, Andy Weil, Victoria Maizes, and all the faculty at the University of Arizona, thank you for training me in the sacred discipline of Integrative Medicine.

To my mentors who encouraged my early interest in Nutrition, Yoga, and Integrative Medicine: Drs. Michael Foley, Curtis Cook, Janet Moore, Doris Derelian, Scott Reaves, and Donald Pinkel, thank you for your support and helping me to be brave enough to have a non-traditional, but incredibly impactful, path in medicine.

To my mother, who bought me my first herbal medicine book by Dr. Low Dog, knowing it would shape my life's work, and to my dad and sister, all of whom have been infinitely supportive of my passionate interest in medicine since childhood. To my proud Grandma Kay who carried my acceptance letter to medical school around in her purse, and to my Grandma Ninna, now with me in Spirit, who loved me dearly just for being me.

To my husband Ryan, who is supportive on a daily basis of my life's work and has encouraged me to pursue every opportunity that has interested me.

And to my little girl, Lillian Jayne, who makes every day new.

Follow me at

www.drannekennard.com

Facebook @drannekennard

IG @dr_anne_kennard

Made in the USA
Las Vegas, NV
11 February 2025